This book is for you if...

- You have major challenges in your life and you are looking for inspiration

- You have received a medical diagnosis that has frightened you

- Your life has been touched by abuse from someone that you trusted

- You want to be reassured that even difficult adversities can be overcome

- You are looking for courage to face what is ahead

What people are saying

'When life gives you lemons, make lemonade' A quote, I am sure, many of you have heard, read or being told to when faced with adversity in life. I personally think that life is not that easy, certainly some days more than others. It pushes us and everyone around us to grow daily while respecting and accepting all its complexity and unpredictability.

This book is a testimony to life and the fight for it. A book, which is written with an open heart that almost leaves nothing left unsaid. As a mother, Mary's story particularly moved and inspired me as I know too well how much my children need me and what I will do and endure in order to make sure I am there for them for as long as I possibly can. However, do not be mistaken. This book is not only for mothers, but also for fighters, believers, disrupters and dreamers. A book that encourages to question the lemons, life so often generously hands out to each and everyone of us, a book that inspires to go the extra mile, a book that fosters a sense of community and belonging in uncertain times.

Dame Tessy Antony de Nassau
Entrepreneur, Philanthropist and Mother

What people are saying

A powerful, captivating testimony of human resilience in the face of multiple life traumas.

Jane McLelland
Award-winning, Bestselling author of ***How To Starve Cancer*** and a Stage IV cancer survivor of 26 years

I think about the impact of releasing the pressure of holding a sad truth and the juxtaposition of liberating ourselves from the shackles of trauma, and in that, the word freedom comes to mind. In life, we face the choice of taking an intrinsic look at our experiences and deciding if we will let our past determine our future or if we are going to choose to live on our terms. Mary's journey is not only one of the personal decisions creating a life of hope, joy, and power but one of choosing freedom from abuse and becoming the hero of her story. This book moved me and reminded me why I always say, though trauma may be our foundation, it is not our future.

Michael Anthony
Childhood abuse survivor
and Author of ***Think Unbroken***

What people are saying

As a childhood sexual abuse survivor myself, Mary's journey strongly resonated with me. I am convinced that this book will reach the heart of many of us. We need to be seen and heard as we have been silenced by fear. Mary is not only giving a voice to her story, but she is also giving a voice to all of us who have been victims for too long. The courage and strength depicted in this book will give hope to many people that life can get better and that they are not defined by what happened to them.

Cali Poulain

Kintsugi is the Japanese art of repairing broken artifacts and treasures. **Cruelly Betrayed** is a beautiful treasure in memoir form. The philosophy behind this type of "repair" is to treat a broken piece of art with care and mend it, providing extra strength and beauty. The repair and healing become part of the artifact's history and value. A broken vase is not thrown out. A repair and mending begin, using gold...No hiding the cracks!

Cruelly Betrayed examines the broken pieces of a tragic childhood and the implications involved with complex trauma. The resilience of the human spirit shines in this carefully crafted book. The value, inspiration, and importance of this beautifully repaired life can only serve as a gift to all who read it.

What people are saying

Mary carefully explores the broken pieces of her life in a vulnerable, realistic, often disturbing way, using words of gold. This book actively encourages the healing process and will help victims of sexual abuse become survivors.

A compelling, realistic, and tumultuous quest to break through extraordinary traumas, release pain, find forgiveness, and healing. It is more than a memoir of a strong and resilient woman. It is truth, forgiveness, healing and empowerment embodied.

Mary's story and ability to paint a realistic picture of abuse has changed me. This is the first time I have been able to understand the fear and hopelessness an abused child faces. This is a story about survival and connection. Not only is she able to connect and inspire survivors but reading this book will help others truly understand the trauma that child abuse, sexual abuse, and familial trauma can cause.

Kimberly King
Award-winning author, Teacher, and Authority on the subject of sexual abuse prevention

Kimberly is the author of the most highly recommended sexual abuse prevention book for children entitled ***I Said No! A kid-to-kid guide to keeping private parts private***

What people are saying

She provides online prevention classes for parents at ***www.kimberlykingbooks.com.*** She has also published a book for children of divorced parents called **When your parents divorce: A kid-to-kid guide to dealing with divorce**

A WORD FROM THE AUTHOR

This book was unplanned. This book was written by accident. This book was typed in the middle of a heavy, still ongoing adversity. It seems that these coming chapters needed to be written to allow the process of emotional healing to begin. The fact that these pages have somehow created themselves within a short time makes me realise that they were brewing inside of me for a long time. They are now ready to be released on paper for me to finally be freed.

My cancer diagnosis has made me face my demons. My cancer has made me look at my life in the eyes and confront my darkest fears. The sequence of events makes me believe that what happens to us is simply a logical consequence of the foundations that are set far back in our childhood by our parents. It is that baseline that will influence our life choices many years down the line. In the face of my own mortality, I came to realise what truly matters in life, which people I do not want around me and which people I really need in my life. I have come to note that this life is volatile, and nothing is guaranteed. It could all be over way too soon. I am only 37 years old and yet have had to endure more hardships than most people around me. Is it simply a strike of bad luck? Is it a natural sequence of events determined by the foundations that my parents gave me or in my case did not give me?

Writing this book without too much effort has shown me that I urgently needed to speak up and stand for myself. I needed to free myself from all this negativity that was eating me up from the inside. I needed to get justice for myself since I had nobody else do it for me, for that little girl inside of me. I needed to feel like I had a voice that was going to be heard, loud and clearly.

Typing page after page, I simply recognised that my life story has a definite 'red thread' throughout, that I did not grasp until I actually wrote chapter after chapter. Are the people we meet in life simply put there by coincidence? Do we attract certain types of people in our life? Do they appear on our path for a deeper purpose, of which we don't know the meaning of until later on in time? The aim of this book was primarily therapeutic for me. For that, the impact of emotional healing has been very intense.

This book is dedicated to my beautiful children, who will always have my truth in a tangible form told with my own words. When they are old enough to read my book, they will undoubtedly feel the love I have for them within the pages. I often tell them that their mother is a superhero, and they will only know what superpowers she harbours when they grow older.

Finally, the last aim of the book is to inspire others who are or have been in my shoes. If I can make it through, you surely can too. We all have that inner force within to keep going no matter what life decides to throw at us. That open door with the light shining through is not far from reach. I am in no way any more special than you. You too can get to the other side of the darkness if you believe that you can.

୰

DEDICATION

This book is dedicated to my beautiful children:
Quentin, Philip, Oliver, Nina and Alexander

With all my love,
Mama

It doesn't matter whether the glass is half full or half empty, at least you still have a glass

ACKNOWLEDGEMENTS

My sweet children, you have been very understanding throughout the past two years despite the constant turbulences in your young lives. My babies give me the daily strength I need to get through any hardship and for this I am very grateful. I am one lucky mummy.

My dear David, you've been my rock when I self-doubted and when I didn't believe I could get through the current storm. You were terrified with me at the horrid news while being overjoyed with me when we received good ones. I feel fortunate to have you in my life.

My lovely Caroline, you caught me when I turned up heavily pregnant in your office. It was only a few days before giving birth, emotionally and physically hurt, at my lowest in a long time. You push me forward and you always manage to say the right things at the right time, and I thank you for that.

My best friend Hild, thank you for being there for me, despite the distance. You are the first person I call, and you have that innate ability to always calm me down. You are my cheerleader from afar.

Madeleine, Faiane, Torugbene, Sonia, Cécilia, Anna Lee thank you for your help and little gestures that made the past months easier on me. I am grateful to have you in my life.

A special thanks to Samantha Houghton and Caroline Emile for their advice and guidance in completing this book.

Cruelly Betrayed

by
Mary Faltz

Published by
Filament Publishing Ltd
16, Croydon Road, Beddington,
Croydon , Surrey CR0 4PA
+44(0)20 8688 2698
www.filamentpublishing.com

Cruelly Betrayed
© 2021 Mary Faltz

ISBN 978-1-913623-41-8

The right to be recognised as the author of this work has been asserted by Mary Faltz in accordance with the Designs and Copyrights Act 1988 Section 77

All rights reserved
No part of this work may be copied without the prior written permission of the publishers

Printed by 4Edge

Disclaimer

Some names have been changed to protect the privacy of individuals. The events in this book are not fictional but are entirely based on a true story. This book contains no medical recommendations.

Contents

1	Who's that woman?	19
2	The power of a smile	27
3	It was too good to be true	85
4	This can't be happening	115
5	The second wave	149
6	Everything will be just fine	171
	Glossary of medical terms	174
	Useful contacts	176

Preface

Do not judge me by my success, judge me by how many times I fell down and got back up again
Nelson Mandela

A question I am being asked quite often as a psychotherapist is: how can you cope hearing so many distressing stories? Isn't this just way too depressing? I could not do the job you do. It is true, that we listen to sad, tragic, shocking and sometimes heart-breaking stories. It is awful what people can do to each other and how much some people have endured.

What most don't know though is that as a psychotherapist you also hear many wonderful, extraordinary and powerful stories. Each and every story is different, and every single client has his or her way to navigate through the storm. What they all seem to have in common is the will to get through and not to cave in, to go on when faced with adversity.

Another idea I often hear is that people who see a psychotherapist are weak and that you can instantly recognize that they are a little off, strange. As a matter of fact, in all the years I have been working I have yet to meet a weak person. The people I saw, have shown amazing strength, courage and a very strong will to persevere. I truly am in awe of them.

As for those people looking a little "off", this is simply not true, quite on the contrary, these people often have an extraordinary façade and you'd never expect the tragedies they faced and have been through.

That does not mean in any way that it is easy to seek help from a psychologist. Anyone who works on their traumas knows how hard these sessions can be and how much courage and patience it takes to face your memories and of course how long it can take to overcome trauma.

Those who find their way into psychotherapist's offices are astonishing people who want to get on with their lives. They want to live and not only survive. They often seek help when their boundaries have been overstepped one too many times, and they just have no more strength left because they have been so strong for such a long time. Asking for help is an upmost important skill, many of us have yet to learn.

What makes my work so gratifying is to see that human beings even if they have had traumatic childhood experiences like physical or emotional abuse, have faced neglect, have lost important people in their lives, have been confronted with natural and human made disasters can be exceptional people. They can be wonderful, sweet, strong and warm parents and know exactly what their child needs. They can be wonderful partners, amazing caregivers, extraordinary friends.

This faculty to rise from hardship, to get going again even when you have been at your lowest is called resilience. The more resilient we are the better we can get through hard times. One way of training our resilience is to look at inspiring people around us, to hear their stories and to pick out those bits that can help us. This person may be your cleaning lady, a teacher, an acquaintance, the man behind the supermarket counter, a VIP person. You can be amazed at how many unknown breath-taking stories there are out there.

One of these unique and extraordinary stories is Mary's and I applaud her for her courage to share it with us.

Caroline Pull
Psychologist and psychotherapist

Chapter One

There's always another story.
There's more than meets the eye.
W.H. Auden

Who's that woman?

From afar, a carefree, loving and smiley mother is pushing a green stroller through the park. The baby is happily playing with his tiny toes. Three young children are holding onto the pushchair, quietly following their mother like a little family of ducklings. The attention from bystanders that this endearing sight provokes is well known to the mother and possibly to the children by now. Be it out of admiration, envy or mere curiosity, the young woman is filled to the brim with pure pride and warm, soft unconditional love when she is out and about with her offspring.

She often receives compliments on how well behaved her children are and that the person saying so could or would, never be able to do such a wonderful job. With a big smile that light up her brown eyes and to the full attention of her children quietly listening, she always replies that she is very fortunate to be their mother. She rarely accepts assistance from well-meaning bystanders or friends. As a highly independent woman, she wants to do it all by herself and seemingly manages very well without any help. From the outside, to many people, this kind woman is a defenceless easy target while her smile is often mistaken for weakness. Appearances can be very deceiving. And yet, behind that glowing face and gentleness, hides a fierce, confident and resilient human being that has immensely endured deep wounding and has rebounded over and over again.

Inevitably, life will not always be a smooth ride for everyone. Many of us will be hit with life changing challenges more than others. Regardless of the obstacle you are going through right now and no matter how insignificant your issue feels compared to others' seemingly more distressing problems, you will get past this. Your pain is not any less important than anyone else's and is just as worthy to be voiced and heard as the traumatic events that I depict in the coming pages. There is no hierarchy when it comes to the subjective suffering. Naturally, it is very difficult to find the slightest positive aspect in the middle of the chaos, but it is there if only you open your eyes to it, making the struggle worthwhile. That little positive in the overall negative will be the one driving force that will keep you going in order to get through the storm. We all carry luggage to a certain extent. No matter whether yours is heavy or on the lighter side, it remains your personal luggage and only you can judge how much suffering it causes you.

Each one of us has a different threshold in dealing with adverse events and it is a shame that there are often comparisons made and opinions on how a person is supposed to feel facing a certain issue. It is entirely up to the person to feel how they need to feel without judgement. I have often wished to be someone else with a seemingly carefree life but at the same time, I would not be who I am today without life's turbulences. I am proud of who I have become in the process and what I have accomplished despite the constant setbacks. I feel truly grateful and fortunate to be surrounded by my beautiful children, who give me every reason to wake up each morning and to take on life's challenges with a smile on my face. We all want to have the lessons and wisdom of life without going through the actual struggle. The two undoubtedly go hand in hand and are positively correlated. The more struggles, the more lessons.

If you are currently going through an adversity of any kind, I recommend that you sit down, take a pen and paper and start writing. The words will start flowing by themselves if you do not judge them as they appear and before you realise it, you will have filled pages out. The soulful action of putting your feelings onto paper is very empowering and symbolic. You transfer them from your heart so that they are released, freeing you up so that you can move on. Keeping these feelings suppressed within you will only cause you further pain. You need to let go of all of this dark heavy negativity to be able to move on to the next happier and more peaceful chapter of your life. You will only find closure when you grasp hold of courage to face your demons instead of keeping them locked away deeply in the drawers of your mind. They will undoubtedly resurface time and time again to relive the same painful expressions. By breaking free from this self-induced prison and unleashing any toxicity that is eating you up from the inside, you gift yourself freedom and peace of mind.

What you do with the pages that you have filled is entirely up to you. You can burn them or take pleasure in tearing them up into shreds so that symbolically they are disposed of. You can keep them locked in a drawer never to be reopened again. You can send them to the people that hurt you without any aim of changing them. And if you feel daring enough, you can even publish those pages for others to read – and who knows, it may even inspire other people to create change in their life. How wonderful would that be? I felt that keeping these pages to myself was not going to do it for me. There was too much suppressed pain, sadness and anger to only talk and share on a one-to-one basis with a therapist. I did not feel it was sufficient in my case.

You will know when you get that urge to publicly uncover your feelings. You will feel the need to share and almost a deep calling, for a purpose greater than yourself. I have been very hesitant about writing and publishing this book. The exposure of deep vulnerability of oneself is very frightening and yet it's an absolute prerequisite in order to embrace change. The therapeutic impact of disclosing my struggles on paper has been substantial and I finally feel at peace to move on to a new chapter of my life, leaving any hard feelings behind. I can't recall how many times I was told 'I wish I were you' over the decades. Likewise, I can't remember the number of times that I wished I was someone else. We often utter these seemingly innocent words without suspecting what may be hiding behind the facade.

We tend to quickly jump to conclusions when we look at a person based on our understanding of the world, through our own lens. Looks can be very deceptive. Smiles can be very deceptive. We associate certain physical characteristics with specific individual behaviours, be it with a positive or a negative label. When we see a man in a smart tailored suit working on a laptop, we make an almost immediate conclusion on his intellectual capacity and professional status. When we notice a man with long hair, wearing a tank top, displaying tattoos on his arms, we also subconsciously make negative assumptions on his character and social status. When we observe a woman wearing heels and red lipstick, we associate her with a powerful dominance. When I wear heels at work, my self-confidence spikes and I behave accordingly. In contrast, when I wear flat shoes at work, I tend to feel like an innocent little girl and not the professional that will be taken seriously. As the saying inspires us to not judge a book by its cover, we should consciously take steps not to categorise people solely by what we see. Be critical when you look at someone as your assumption may be entirely wrong about that person and you may miss opportunities to discover who that person really is.

With the writing of this book, I no longer wish I was someone else but proudly stand tall in the midst of a storm. I am allowing myself to be vulnerable and by doing so, wholeheartedly embrace the valuable lessons that are given to me through adversity. The world is frightening and yet beautiful at the same time. We have a choice in determining how we interpret it. Beauty being in the eye of the beholder stands very true in this case. Nevertheless, in the eye of misfortune, we should welcome the feelings of fear, sadness and anger. They have their justified roles and should in no way be dismissed. They form a natural part of the process. Managing these feelings appropriately in order for them not to flood each waking (and sleepless) moment should be the ultimate aim.

Regardless of your motivation for holding my book between your hands, I wish that you find comfort in reading what I share upon the pages. If I can encourage you to open your eyes to what truly makes your life worthwhile, then the purpose of this book will have been fulfilled. You have deep inside of you all that it takes to believe that you can make it through. No matter how unsurmountable the situation seems to be right now, have faith that this is not your final destination. You will find strength to survive the hardship of any adversity that life has cast in your direction. Not only will you survive, but you will come out of it stronger than ever and thrive to also tell the tale.

As I am writing this, I am in the midst of turbulence and therefore have a long way ahead of me in order to learn how to manage these feelings. I am convinced that as time heals, I will also be able to see the world with a ratio of frightening to beautiful of 30/70 and not 70/30. Baby steps.

The Power of Conditioning

Chapter Two

*I can be changed by what happens to me,
but I refuse to be reduced by it.*
Maya Angelou

The power of a smile.

The walls are white and cold. The building feels intimidating to someone unfamiliar to the legal world. Sitting in the corner at the entrance of the High Court of Justice, I feel very defeated. I feel my baby kicking in response to my distress. Suddenly, the sound of the clicking of handcuffs from afar draws my attention. I turn around and see two armed policemen taking him away into a shielded police van. I watch as the van is slowly driving off into the distance. I need to make sure that he really is gone. The sigh of relief, watching this scene play out in front of me is immense.

My life, as far as I can remember, has always been atypical, although the beginnings seemed quite ordinary in a small town by the river Moselle in Luxembourg. I am the second born and eldest daughter out of six children. Just like regular siblings, one could not have been any more different than the next born. The bungalow we lived in was overlooking a big, lovely garden with a wooden swing and a green plastic slide, which in turn was facing the calm river. My family was highly educated and with both parents working in the medical field, it was a firm given that I was expected to follow that same career path.

From the outside, the family of eight did not seem particularly striking although the mere fact of there being eight people in one household was eye-catching enough. My father Nicolas, the patriarch of the family, was effortlessly running the show. He is short, far-sighted and likes his coffee black. The internal task distribution in our home was traditional and my mother Nelly was assigned the seamless execution of the daily household chores. Nelly does not like loud music nor dogs. My older brother Andreas has dark wavy hair, a gap between his front teeth and big brown eyes. He loved playing basketball although he was not particularly tall. My younger sister Denise is short, has brown curly hair, small eyes and thin lips. She is always right and never gets punished. She is also known as 'Miss Perfect' within the family. The fourth born child was Leonard. He is the 'Computer man' of the bunch. He would spend hours on end in front of the computer screen and was always willing to fix any technical issues. He is short, wears glasses and likes donuts. Elena is tall, curvy and has an intimidating frizzy hairdo. She is very confident and likes to imitate animal sounds. She was regarded as the 'Conflict solver'.

The last-born child, Mira lacks confidence and a front tooth. Despite that imperfection, she was always seen as the doll of the family. She would display a picture ready duck face at all times, just in case a camera was close by. As for me, I was rather shy and clumsy, yet funny. I am not at ease around free walking animals and I like drinking from a straw to keep my teeth white. I value good manners and have always liked my first name; my mother chose well. My thigh gap was strangely envied by my three sisters. I had to grow up quickly to become the responsible member of the lot. I was unpopularly considered to be 'Miss Know-it all'.

During her prime years, my mother was a pretty, tall and slim woman with long curly dark brown hair, beautiful hazel eyes and a timid smile. She was very bright and of a calm nature. After obtaining her medical degree, she got engaged to Chris; a tall, handsome aerospace engineer with glasses whom she loved dearly and envisaged herself sharing her future with. She had her life planned out with Chris. They would travel for a couple of years before settling down into serious life. Nelly was very keen on moving away and finally leaving her small birth town. She wanted to see the world before having children. Her wedding date was set, the 27th January 1980. It was going to be a big, beautiful wedding as Nelly had planned it in her mind since she was a little girl. The wedding dress was bought, the guests were invited, the slot for the church ceremony booked, the catering was ordered, the decorations were ready and all that was missing was the bride and the groom.

As the wedding day got closer, Nelly felt herself getting more and more excited about finally getting married and leaving the family nest. Shortly before the wedding date, Chris asked to speak to the bride's father in person. The groom to-be, nervously approached Nelly's family home. He was greeted as usual with a warm welcome by his soon to-be parents in law. There was no right way of saying what was on his mind. Chris indeed got cold feet. He apologised and confirmed his wish to cancel the wedding. Nelly was listening from afar. She could not believe that the man she had pictured spending her next life chapter with, had not only broken her heart but also immensely humiliated her this close to the wedding day. The parents in law were very angry and upset by this decision and for obvious reasons despised Chris for hurting, not only their daughter's feelings but also their reputation as a family.

During the days that followed, Nelly isolated herself in her room and did not wish to speak to anyone. She refused to eat and was slowly falling into a depression. She felt anger, disappointment, sadness and embarrassment as any woman would feel if the love of her life decided to stand her up this close to a wedding that was ready to be celebrated. She was also mourning the opportunity to finally leaving the family home and travelling away. One of the invited wedding guests was Nicolas. He was a simple acquaintance to Nelly. She only knew him from a distance. He was involved in church and was a scout when he was younger. He was well appreciated within his family and circle of friends. Always ready to joke but philosophical at the same time. He would recite Bible verses and make sense of them in real life situations. Nicolas was not particularly good looking. He did not wear glasses and therefore looked less intellectual than Chris. Nicolas was the same height as Nelly. Unlike Nelly, he did not have a queue of admirers waiting at his front door. He loved travelling and he had been working abroad for years. He seemed open minded.

A few days after Chris visited to announce his reluctance to marry Nelly, Nicolas dropped by Nelly's house to try and comfort her. What Nelly did not know until then is that Nicolas had been fancying her since they were children. He never dared declaring his love to her but somehow found a golden opportunity in the midst of Nelly's heartbreak. Nelly refused to see him, she was not keen on talking to anyone and certainly not to him. Time needed to pass for her to enjoy life again. Nevertheless, Nicolas persuaded her to open her bedroom door and let him in. Nicolas did not hesitate one moment. After comforting her and letting Nelly know that what Chris did to her was heartless and selfish, he jumped on the opportunity to propose to her a deal which she simply could not refuse. He suggested to her that she should keep the wedding date with all the arrangements and instead of marrying Chris, she should marry him. They would un-invite the guests on Chris' side and invite further guests on short notice from Nicolas' family and circle of friends.

He went on and let her know how much she meant to him since they were children and that he had never forgotten her throughout the years. Nelly was shocked to say the least but that love declaration did not help her in any way get over losing the love of her life. She was speechless and overwhelmed by the offer. On the one hand, it would be a chance for her to finally escape the small village she grew up in but on the other hand, it just did not feel right to marry someone she did not love. Could she really be happy in that arrangement and perhaps fall in love with Nicolas after the wedding? For Nelly, the deal sounded very business-like. She was torn between her principles and her dreams. She finally agreed to the arrangement and the wedding went ahead as planned. Albeit with only half of the originally invited guests and a new group of invitees from Nicolas' side.

During the first years of marriage, Nicolas cherished Nelly and treated her like a royalty. The feelings on Nelly's side towards Nicolas were very different. Whether she ever developed feelings for this man will always remain a mystery. She was happy with the deal she had made a few years prior but how long for? With each child that she gave birth to, she slowly realised that this is not the life that she had wished for herself. She could not get herself to be a loving, nurturing and affectionate mother as was expected of her. She could not imagine herself playing that role and slowly withdrew herself from family life. Nicolas noticed a change in her behaviour shortly after Mira was born. He could not understand why Nelly was struggling, he had given her the perfect life after all. Nicolas became nervous when Nelly started to deeply question her marriage to him and became more and more unhappy as the months passed.

Up to this day, I do not know what diagnosis would have been appropriate for what my mother was going through. She was trapped. She found herself marrying this man out of desperation and had six children to raise. She never wanted that life and so she started showing signs of rebellion. She started digging into the past and mentioned names of random men. She was searching for answers. Nicolas quickly quietened that urge in her. He did it by verbal and physical means, both as painful as the other I suspect. For as long as I can recall, Nelly was admitted in and out of the psychiatric hospital. It became almost a saddened ritual as Nicolas would call the police every once in a while, and they would turn up with an ambulance to whisk Nelly away for a few months at a time. Nicolas would always find a valid reason for her to be escorted by physical force out of the family home, it was never a quiet affair. I remember him being angry about the ambulance bill because they mostly had to come on the weekends and so the bill was higher than normal.

Nicolas would brief the six children to blatantly lie to the psychiatrist of the hospital into claiming that Nelly had done wrong yet again so that she would easily be admitted and rather cruelly kept out of his way. He told us to repeat a script that he had prepared to support his case, with seemingly no guilt or pangs of conscience. We made Nelly look like an unfit mother as per his request. I wouldn't go as far as giving her the 'Mother of the year' award, but she never deserved that treatment by her husband. He seemed to want to get rid of her at any cost, as she was a burden to him at that point.

Examples of 'acts', my mother needed to be punished for are described in the following sentences. She inappropriately mixed incompatible food ingredients together which did not conform to her husband's taste buds. She once put too much salt in the food. She once mixed the coloured and white laundry with the obvious outcome of pink shirts. Nicolas seemingly did not like that colour on him. She once moved the furniture in the living room without her husband's approval. She once forgot Andreas in the supermarket and went home. This indeed may sound dramatic but who can blame her with six children? At least she called a taxi to pick him up after realising she had only come home with five children. Andreas does not seem to have any residual emotional scar from that particular incident.

My mother used to write letters to her deceased father which, in Nicolas' eyes, was apparently a sign of being disconnected from reality and hence worthy of another in-patient psychiatric stay. Our father made it clear to us that our mother was unlike other mothers and that she was 'sick'. We simply obeyed as children do, believing that our father knows best, innocently not realising that it meant that our mother would be gone for a few months again.

I soon learnt that if I didn't conform to my father's expectations, my future would look the same, locked up on a bleak and lonely psychiatric ward. It was my word against an adult's word after all – who would believe the child? Nicolas would drag up old records from the past, 'proving' that Nelly's great grandmother

Bethany was schizophrenic. That was the starting point for him to convince multiple psychiatrists over a span of three decades, that his wife was mentally disturbed. He would also instruct her to continue to pretend to be 'sick' in front of the doctors in order for her to continue receiving an incapacity pension. I don't know how much was planned and how much was improvised. It was obviously a realistic performance for the professionals to repeatedly swallow the charade.

Nicolas was very dominant over his wife. She was fully at his mercy without questioning any of it, she had no voice of her own left. She had surrendered a long time ago and defencelessly embraced this 'victim' image. She wore it convincingly. Sometimes, Nicolas would pretend that we were going on a family trip and my mother unwittingly would do as she was told and simply get in the car. Little did she know that her husband was actually driving her to the psychiatric hospital for another in-patient stay. He had prepared her suitcase with her belongings, placed it in the car, tricking her all over again.

My mother was physically absent during most of my childhood. She spent more time in the psychiatric hospital than at home. Nicolas hired many nannies over the years, too many to even remember. They were supposed to help him care for his six children. Unsurprisingly, many of them accused him of sexual assault decades later. Since I was used to Nicolas telling me every detail of his cheating adventures with random women, I was not shocked by the accusations. When my mother was back at home, she was physically present but was dosed up on such heavy medication that she could not do anything for herself, let alone think clearly. The image that I have left of her, portrays a tired, pale woman with a hair bun, sitting on the sofa, watching TV and fully disconnected from real life. She would be in this dreadful vegetative state for months on end. She did not show any emotions or rational thinking. She would regularly be topped up with her neuroleptic depot injections that would keep her alive but totally dead on the inside.

When I was growing up, life seemed pretty normal in those early days. I was quite a tomboy and I was not remotely into dolls, pink or glitter. I was the only girl in a boys only football team. I was put in an attacker's position thanks to my quick tackling skills. I absolutely loved getting the ball from the opposing team and passing it on for someone else to score. I rarely scored a goal myself. I was respected by the boys in the team and that felt great. From an early age, I tried to override my shy nature with humour and quickly found my place with this strategy. Three decades later, this strategy is still in place and functioning well.

When I was nine years old, my mother was yet again away on one of her many stays at the psychiatric hospital. My father was solely in charge of the management of six children including a baby. One evening, after dinner and bath, he put the younger children to bed, and I was left to take my bath on my own. He blew dried my long dark hair that was reaching up to my lower back. Up until that particular evening, Nicolas had never paid attention to me, I was simply one of his six children and that was very right by me. I didn't feel any different to my siblings nor to my peers at school. On that evening, unexpectedly, Nicolas, at some point decided to step beyond his moral boundaries while maintaining his authority figure. That same night was the first time he entered my bedroom, came into my bed and molested me.

Over the years that followed, I remained vigilant at night, each and every night. The dreaded creaking of the wooden stairs in the middle of the night and my bedroom door squeaking while slowly being opened, kept me awake every single night. What made this man, an apparent good Christian with moral principles without a drop of alcohol in his blood, consciously take action to do wrong is a big question mark to me. Was it planned? Was it driven by an opportunistic sexual impulse? Was he doing that to my other siblings too? As a child, I often wondered whether both of my parents were actually mentally sick. By then, I had already believed that my mother was not like other mothers, convinced by what Nicolas, the family and the doctors said. I, however, also started to question whether my father was like other fathers.

I would go to school with little sleep, if at all, and still be able to function and score high grades. My internal system seemed to radically accommodate what was happening to me in order for me to cope and to unconsciously carry on as normal. When she was home, my mother seemed to realise what was going on in her more lucid moments, but never once questioned it and did not take steps to protect her child from harm. This abuse went on for SIXTEEN long and painful years behind closed doors in harrowing silence.

As time passed, the abuse got more extensive and my father didn't hesitate to even touch me in broad daylight, often in the presence of my mother and siblings. It did not surprise anyone that I elbowed our father or vigorously slapped his hands off me. It seemed to me that whatever behaviour, if one makes sure that it is normalised then it is casually accepted by everyone even if it loses all sense of morality. It therefore did not shock anyone that my father casually touched my breasts under my shirt or had his hand between my legs in broad daylight on the sofa while everyone else is living around us, including my own mother.

At every opportunity, he would make me sit on his lap, whether I was 9 or 17 while he'd be sexually aroused, and I'd be so disgusted that I'd go away. He always got me back. I had no free will like my siblings, they were very lucky in my eyes. As the years passed, the acceptance of the abuse reached a point where Nicolas would force me in broad daylight to go upstairs to my bedroom, lock the door behind us and freely abuse me. In one of her police testimonies, my mother told the investigating officer that she did not see any harm in a father trying to French kiss his daughter. There seemed to be a certain consensus in this family, a very distorted one but very much existent. Whenever he was alone with me, without exception, each and every time, he would force me to lift my shirt up to show my naked breasts to him.

Since he had seen that what he was doing did not seem to surprise anyone, he started abusing me in our jacuzzi, this all while my siblings were also in the bubbly water next to us. It all became just 'normal' for everyone. He seemed to gain confidence with time passing that nobody was alerted to what was happening. My father always talked about penis, vagina and breasts as being nothing special, that they bear the same value as an arm, leg or foot. Sexual abusers often do so in order for the child to feel comfortable touching the abuser's genitals and vice versa.

The fact that any morality is removed by normalising any sexual reference gives free access to the molester. My father's sex talk became part medical part sexual. He told me that I was his 'patient' that needed help. He would always insist that I sit on the passenger seat in the car next to him so he could start his sex talk, often while having his hand between my leg or trying to go under my shirt. For as long as I can remember, I have lived 16 years slapping and elbowing this man in a desperate attempt to push his dirty hands off my body. He would angrily tell me to stop because 'what would my mother and siblings say if they saw the marks on him?'. He remained physically stronger than me throughout the years.

Sometimes, he would be so furious at me for hurting him that he wouldn't talk to me for a few days, while also punishing me. He would take things away from me or forbid me to do activities that he had previously given his permission for. Those angry episodes of him were very fine by me because I then knew that during these days, I would not receive the nightly visits. This punishment never lasted longer than two days before he came back to make 'peace' with me and the nightly visits resumed to my absolute horror. I often pretended to have my period when it was not the case, in an attempt to deter him from touching me. To my absolute disgust, this excuse did not prevent him in any way.

When the abuse first happened, I was sharing a bedroom with three of my siblings. That did not worry Nicolas. Later on, I shared a room with only one sibling before I had my own room. I remember that my room was adjacent to Denise's room, only separated with a door behind which was my bed. When Nicolas would visit me on a nightly basis, I would kick that door with my foot to make noise in the hope that someone would wake up and interrupt the abuse. Nicolas would tell me to stop before waking everyone up. He used to tightly hold my foot in order to prevent me from kicking that door. Where were the other 6 people in the house while I was helplessly succumbing day and night for years to this disgusting man?

I often went to my mother in bed in order not to be touched. What was I thinking? Even then, he would follow me and lie next to me on the other side, away from my mother and touched me as usual, fully ignoring her presence. Since my mother took sleeping pills, Nicolas was pretty sure she would be fast asleep. She never intervened when I was blatantly being molested in broad daylight so I guess I would not have expected any other reaction had she noticed the abuse happening right there next to her in bed. I feel like I have spent 16 years awake, constantly running away from this man to an empty bed or sofa to try and get some sleep. He would always follow me.

When my mother was home, Nicolas insisted that I join them in the bedroom to watch them having sexual intercourse. That seemed insufficient, so Nicolas forced me to join in despite my disgusted reluctance. He insisted I stay on the bed while both of them were naked on top of each other. This again, was a so called 'learning experience' for my own good. He often asked me to get whipped cream and I had to put it on my mother's breasts. While I was being a forced spectator of my parents' sex life, I was very jealous of my siblings being allowed to have a carefree childhood on the other side of the locked bedroom that I found myself in. Nicolas would always make sure that he locks the bedroom door and put the key up high so I could not reach it to leave the room. Even if I could have run away, where to? He would always get what he wanted from me with his ever-increasing age-appropriate threats.

From the early days of the abuse, Nicolas started speaking in codes with me. He would give childish nicknames to genitals and breasts. His penis was called 'Lola' for example. He could then freely talk about this in front of anyone without any suspicion that it was purely sexual. This way it all became a game, and the sexual reference was removed in his mind. But not in mine. I felt disgusted, dirty, ashamed and lived in constant, absolute fear of my own father in my own home. I absolutely hated my childhood, adolescence and young adulthood.

If this is hell, then I was certainly in the middle of it and there was no way out. I was trapped and this man had all the power over me. He was obsessed with my being, partly for his own pleasure and partly, which I can only imagine was fear of me speaking out. I can't imagine that he was not scared of his dirty secret coming out one day and him being in huge trouble. He smartly made me believe all these years that if 'our' secret comes out that I would be the one punished and not him. I would be the one sent to prison. He had often threatened to send me to a youth shelter if I didn't conform. I had of course seen how easy it was for him to regularly get rid of my mother with one simple telephone call.

I had no other choice than to believe what he was saying was true. He was the adult after all, and I had nobody else to tell me that the opposite was true. He made sure I remained ignorant. Whenever I read about 'sexual abuse' in my teen magazine; for my own survival, I always justified to myself that I was not concerned. I convinced myself that sexual abuse is always linked to violence and what my own father was doing was 'medical' after all and in no way sexual. I don't know what it is like to enjoy carefree years with unconditional care and love from parents. I have never had a chance to experience that pure love that I am fortunate enough to give to my own children today.

Whenever I innocently asked my father when he would stop, he used to answer that he will stop when I prove to him that I enjoy what he was doing as that would mean to him that the learning experience was successful. Apparently, that would be my 'graduation'. His exact words were: 'I need to see an angel smile on your face'. I let you figure out what he meant by that. All he received from my face during these 16 horrid years, however, were tears, fear and absolute disgust. He even used to tell me that he will still continue even when I have my own children. He said that he will drink my breastmilk from the source after giving birth. That disgusting affirmation was enough for me to not ever want to have children of my own when I was younger. All this was happening in my parallel world while other children my age were enjoying their happy childhood. I was sadly very envious.

Over the years, I had perfected my smile behind which was hidden a painful double life. I was closely being watched in order not to raise any suspicions about the abuse. What would have happened if I had not pretended everything was fine? I dare not imagine. There were plenty of silent cries for help and hints of the abuse, but nobody spoke openly or took any action, neither within nor outside the family. Nicolas was a charismatic Christian figure that compared himself to God. He was respected and admired for his apparent generosity and kindness. Appearances can be deceptive.

Out of six children, I would often travel around the world with Nicolas on his business trips. I would go to far away places with him including Tokyo, Hong Kong, Macau, Singapore, Toronto, Los Angeles and Dubai. He always made sure that we receive one double bed and not two single beds when asked at the hotel reception, to the surprise of the employee since I was already a teenager and later on a young adult. I often felt like the hotel reception employees must have thought that I was not his daughter but some sort of escort/prostitute that he rented out for his pleasure. He often made me watch pornographic movies with him in the hotel room. I was fully at his mercy, far away from my home although even in my own home I never felt safe.

I was made out to be the special one and I would receive an endless stream of presents while the other five siblings would be dismissed and disadvantaged. They usually received my old belongings that I no longer used. This open favouritism by Nicolas towards me only produced feelings of guilt and shame in me – they were my brothers and sisters and nothing about the situation felt right nor made any sense, it only separated me further. All I was craving at the time was connection to my siblings and to feel loved and safe as any child would. When I was ten years old, Nicolas, as deranged as he was, brought about 30 sexy satin underwear from Hong Kong for me to wear along with an expensive breast firming lotion by *Clarins*.

I long hesitated whether to disclose examples of the abuse in this book but came to the conclusion that if I wanted to contribute to prevention then I need to point out the red flags in order to recognise sexual predators and paedophiles by unravelling their mechanisms of action. The more we raise awareness of the presence of these disgusting men and women in our society, the more we will make potential abusers think twice before they contemplate putting their dirty hands on a child.

I was treated like a princess and always placed on a pedestal by Nicolas for being the good obedient student and his pretty daughter that he loved to show off. The healthy boundaries between a father and daughter were completely destroyed. Nicolas' behaviour indirectly enraged and created jealousy in my siblings from an early age, quite understandably so – who would not object to this special treatment to one child and not the others? At primary and later in secondary school, the other children would envy me and 'wish they were me' as they saw how well travelled I was and the lavish gifts I was spoilt with over and over again. In my head, I wish I could have told them that I was imprisoned and so desperately unhappy. If only they knew of the dark truth, they would not have felt this way towards me.

Despite Nicolas' apparent care to me, he was surprisingly also physically very brutal, which was very confusing to be on the receiving end of, especially when I was being violated by my very own father. Interestingly, he spared the four younger siblings and only Andreas, my mother and myself had to endure his loss of temper. Nicolas was cruel. He would take a fork or a spoon and put it in the open fire or on the stove and then viciously force it on our bare skin to burn us. He seemed to derive pleasure from his vile actions. When I was four years old, I refused to finish eating the scrambled eggs on my plate. Nicolas grabbed a fork, put it in the fire until it was extremely hot and burnt the top of my hand with it. I felt the scalding singe on my flesh and screamed with pain as he did so. I have lived on with that fork scar on my hand as a visual reminder of his brutality. Not all scars were as visible. Andreas had quite a few remarkable burn marks on his body that he seemed to have forgotten the origin of. Maybe it was his memory shutting down to protect him?

Nicolas was very aggressive with his wife and he used to tie her up with ropes to the radiators for her not to defend herself. She once pulled his testicles in self-defence, which I was very pleased about to say the least, not only to witness her standing up for herself but for him to experience some of his own treatment in return. I have a vivid memory of being on a family trip on the Belgian Coast. I must have been about eight as Mira was still a baby at the time. In the hotel room, Nicolas ordered Nelly to change Mira's diapers, to which she replied that he should do it. He quickly lost his temper and while changing Mira, he scooped up her stools out of her sodden diaper and stuffed them in my mother's mouth by force. As if that was not humiliating enough, he proceeded to wickedly hitting her with a keyring that held a bunch of keys on her thighs until she was black and blue and howling and whimpering in pain.

Life continued and so did the nightly abuse. The survival instinct was in full action and no matter how much I defended myself, I had absolutely no chance against an adult. With each questioning, my father would age appropriately justify his actions to me by saying it's educational, medical or plain normal. I was very confused. Did my father love me? Was I really special? Did he just use me? How did he justify this abuse in his head for him to feel like it was righteous? How could he love me if he was doing me wrong at the same time? Why did I need to be the special one? How I wished to be another sister who could sleep through the night. How I wished to not be scared every single night. I developed hatred for this man while everyone else loved him. I knew his real face and I had to keep quiet and keep on smiling. Despite me slapping and scratching him to defend myself, he was always stronger than me.

When I had reached the age of fourteen, I lost ten kilograms within a short space of time, yet nobody seemed to be bothered or notice this cry for help. I felt invisible to the world and the people in it. Consciously or unconsciously, I did not want to have any of the feminine assets that puberty brought to me. My period stopped, my breasts disappeared, and I was surviving on just one slice of bread a day. The physical, sexual and psychological abuse continued, and nobody was alarmed to what was going on, not the teachers nor the family. No one seemed to spot any signs of distress within me and I dare not speak out. I was left alone to succumb to the suffering that this disgusting man enforced onto me each day. Nobody wondered or questioned as to why he would wake up in the morning in my bed, his daughter's bed, nobody thought twice, it became just the normal routine. All quite unbelievable to consider that this could actually happen within a family.

The years passed, the abuse continued, and I was living a horrid double life. During the day, I was functioning on very little sleep, the adrenaline chugging throughout my body must have kept me wired in survival mode. I was fitting in with my peers, I had Backstreet boys posters on my walls, fancied B-Rok and consistently bought a German teen magazine called *Bravo* every Thursday for 52 Luxembourgish Francs. I was an overachiever, scoring high grades and smiling on the outside. I convincingly wore my mask that hid my pain all too well. Then I became terrified at night of that horrible and sickening man coming into my room.

Sexual predators are rarely people outside of the family, they sugar coat the abuse during the years that they act on their depraved desires, conditioning their victim from a young age that this is what fathers, or whoever they may be, do. As I matured and became more aware, I was able to realise more and more that the abuse was not 'normal', yet I never told anyone for 16 years out of the most profound fear and shame that gnawed into my psyche, but I continually pushed it away, in order to maintain the secret. Had I spoken out, the potential consequences of what may happen to me then, felt too much for me to even comprehend.

I had seen how my father was capable of imprisoning my mother for months at a time in a psychiatric hospital. She had no voice. It was the precise projection of what may happen to me if I had gone against someone like him. What if it made everything much worse? How would I deal with that? I could clearly imagine the fury of my father, as I pictured his angry face in my mind and heard the wrath in his voice. And who would believe me, against his words? What if I somehow found the courage to tell somebody and they didn't believe what I said? There was also the strange feeling that I would be betraying my father and how could I do that? It was easier and better that I kept quiet. It somehow must be my fault after all, so I convinced myself.

Since the early days of the abuse, I used to ask Nicolas why he touched me and not the other sisters. His replies were always as such that the other sisters did not 'need' that. I was, according to him, the shy and ugly one out of his four daughters and that I needed to 'get out of myself'. According to him, the other three were open minded girls and I was 'special' and different. He used to say that they were comfortable with their body while I always hid my chest with my long hair because I was extremely shy. How could I ever be comfortable with my body that he misused for his own pleasure? This man broke my self-esteem before it even had a chance to develop in a healthy way. I apparently needed more 'help'. Many years later, Nicolas' defence during the criminal trial was that, out of all of his children, I was the only one to have inherited my mother's 'mental illness' and that is why I obviously needed more attention. Needless to say, that the judges did not fall for that.

As the secret should remain between us, my father told me that 'others wouldn't understand'. To help me cope, as although I pushed a lot of my feelings down, they were always emerging to haunt me, I started looking for foundations with the aim of cleansing myself. Very early on, I prayed daily, and I would go to church on my own and confess for what I had done with this strong belief that I was the culprit. It felt like my church visits gave me the clean consciousness that I needed to survive. It seemed that by going every week, the abuse was erased, albeit temporarily. Week after week, this warped cycle continued. I felt very dirty as if I had done something wrong. I was forgiven each week. How could the world of a little girl become so distorted by the actions of a deranged man? My mother was unimpressed with my weekly church visits and used to ridicule me for attending. I felt quite out of place in church. Apart from me, there was always this Portuguese neighbour who kneeled on the floor and a few other older people. The only other young people that I would see on a weekly basis would be the few that were forced to go by their parents and the acolytes.

The abuse was neatly and conveniently packaged and presented to me as presents, care and love. It was always age appropriately justified as a 'learning experience' in order to 'know how to treat men later' or 'that all fathers do that'. I could not understand how an authority figure that is supposed to love and protect could do this much disgusting harm to their child. I experienced many feelings of conflict, as parts of me felt it was wrong but parts of me believed it was justified because Nicolas is a caring parent after all. I continued to function and score the best grades on very little sleep that enabled me to survive.

I keenly moved to the UK for my studies and hoped that the physical distance would stop the abuse, but Nicolas followed me there. He hired a private detective in order to track my every move and monitor every person that I was in contact with, who was then thoroughly investigated and threatened away. Nicolas was obsessed with my person and no-one else was allowed access to me. I was his possession and if I did not do as I was told, he would threaten me in the most horrible ways. Many years had passed by then, the conditioning of that little girl was still working on her as a young adult and he gained full control. On the outside, I appeared to be an independent, smiley, educated, fully functioning healthcare professional.

The reality behind the mask was very different. This deranged man had full control of my every move and the people I was in contact with – he was running the show.

During my first year of studies, I had met a handsome and kind man through a Luxembourgish online Quiz forum. Luke has green eyes, a big smile and is an eloquent speaker. He often eats chocolate croissants for dinner and does not like exotic fruits. Up until then, I had not experienced what it was like to be in a relationship with a man. Despite being miles away, Luke was very affectionate and gave me all the attention that a woman could ever wish for. He was very thoughtful and put a great amount of work into making sure I was feeling pretty and loved. He never ceased to surprise me on special occasions. This was very unfamiliar to me. I was not used to an honest, romantic and respectful type of relationship. I did not give Luke that same attention back as I was overwhelmed and perhaps doubtful as to Luke's true intentions. I had, up until then, only known my body to be misused for someone else's pleasure and did not understand that a man could truly love me for me. Soon, Nicolas discovered the relationship and questioned me about it. He wanted to know every detail although, unbeknownst to me, he already had all the answers by accessing my email accounts, diverting my text messages to his phone and through the reporting of the private detective. There was no room for lying even if I tried. He would always know better.

One day, I travelled back to Luxembourg and visited Luke, of course after Nicolas authorised me to. I needed to give him the exact time and place and during each of my encounters with Luke, my father would call me and ask me to speak to him. He was very present in our relationship. It felt like he was part of it. I never felt free in this relationship as it was driven and watched by my father. It was as if I did not have control at all as my every move, as well as every spoken and written word was supervised. A few months into the relationship, Nicolas asked to meet Luke's parents. I did not want that, but my father insisted it was either that or I could never see Luke ever again. Having no other choice, I reluctantly told Luke, who was just as surprised at the request as I was.

The day had come, it was a bright summer day and my father made me drive to Luke's house. His mother opened the door, also surprised at this strange meet and greet. She had not met me until that day and was obviously also wondering what this woman was doing in their house bringing along her father. She had prepared coffee and cake and kindly invited us in. Luke's father was sat opposite us and Nicolas proceeded to talk about random topics. I was embarrassed to say the least and the feeling of being kept hostage was very well known to me. The impression of not being able to be myself because someone else is controlling my movement and speech was very familiar. It's as if I never knew what it was like to not be a puppet on a string and have that freedom that people at my age take for granted. How I wished I was a free adult at the time.

During the conversation, Nicolas started deviating from the small talk and went straight into the sex talk. He raised his voice and started educating Luke on how if he ever gets me pregnant that he will need to take full responsibility and that raising a child was not easy as he had raised six children by himself. At that moment, I just wanted to hide under the table. I could not believe that my father was continuing with his sex talk as if that was a common thing to do on a first encounter with a new boyfriend's parents. I profusely apologised to Luke and hoped that this strange meeting would not chase him away as Nicolas had obviously hoped. Luke admitted that this was all out of order, but that he still loved me and that he could ignore what had happened.

A few years had passed, and Nicolas was feeling threatened by Luke's increasing presence in my life, but he was somehow pleased that I was 'locked' in a relationship that was long distance. This way, I could not date someone physically in the UK and I would not physically see Luke on a regular basis. Perhaps he sensed that his secret may slowly come out? He was very uncomfortable with my relationship with Luke. When it got more serious, Nicolas instructed me to break up with Luke. He told me if I didn't, he would make sure that he'd damage Luke's reputation and speak to his parents. I was 23 at the time. I had nothing to say, no joker to be used. All I could do was obey. I then wrote a long letter to Luke, breaking up with him and apologising that it was me, not him. The letter was read and validated by Nicolas. I reassured Luke that he did nothing wrong and that any girl that would be with him would be very lucky. I felt very imprisoned at an age at which young adults are free and taking their own decisions, driving where they want, when they want to. I wished I was one of them. Luke's reaction was obviously one of shock, anger and sadness. He told me that I had just played with his feelings and he made me feel like I was a bad person. I accepted it, not being able to tell him the truth as nobody would believe me.

After years of abuse, my own body image evidently suffered. I was not taught the healthy foundations or boundaries that I needed to respect my body. I felt that my body had betrayed me. I was under the impression that the only reason I was being abused was because my body decided to display feminine traits at an early age which made me incredibly self-conscious. I really wished that I was a boy. At the age of 12, I quickly blossomed out and became big chested while the rest of my body remained slim. I remember my mother shouting at me from her regular sofa spot and humiliating me in front of everyone when I told her that I got my first period. For as long as I can remember, I tried very hard to hide my chest. When the same breasts have been the reason why an adult started to abuse you, you develop a disgust and hatred towards your own body. I never embraced being a girl.

During my studies, I consciously decided to get into serious weightlifting. The original aim was to reduce my chest size, which did not happen as the breasts are made up of fat tissue. The familiar image of female bodybuilders losing female traits greatly motivated me to continue with this unusual hobby. The obsession was intense and for years, I spent every free minute before and after work, at the gym lifting weights. Having a smaller chest size consumed every waking moment as I convinced myself that this would make everything better. My whole thinking was focused on how to ingest 100 grams of protein per day and the guilt that I felt if I missed out on lifting one day was immense. I took supplements and whey protein to increase muscle mass quickly. It became a very unhealthy habit but somehow gave me some control of the situation. It felt good to look 'strong' and it gave me an inner strength. It is very easy to fall into such a vicious cycle, no matter what activity.

Over the years, my father's threats became more and more intense and I would fear for my life. Nicolas was two faced and his façade continued, never slipping. On the outside, he was a caring father and a generous Christian, yet only I knew his other dark disgusting side, but I couldn't share it with anyone. I grew up with so much disgust towards this man. I was alone with it, for years, that little girl was left to fight on her own, every single night. No matter how much resistance I would give him, he remained stronger physically and psychologically and had full control. I was entirely at his mercy and nobody could help me. They didn't even know for goodness sake. That's how tragic and pathetic it was.

Nicolas even found new coercive methods to control and abuse me as an adult. Despite being a highly educated professional, Nicolas would force me to transfer all of my salary to his account so that I would have very little money left, and just enough to fill my tank so that I could drive to work every day. He made me financially dependent on him with my own money. He diverted all of my calls and messages to his phone and was aware of my every move and communications either by stalking me physically or through the information the detective would provide him with. He often showed up in the UK with no prior warning and threatened people that I was in contact with to leave me alone or he would harm their reputation in one way or another. I always made sure to save any boy's name under an invented girl's name in my phone, even at the age of 26.

During my first year abroad, the detective had provided Nicolas with 'secrets' about my newly made friends. One day, I returned to my flat, only to find Nicolas sitting there around a table with all my friends. I had no idea what was happening. All I could do was innocently watch as my father was threatening each one of them that he would tell their parents about whatever 'secret' they had if they remained in contact with me. I was speechless, embarrassed and as very familiar to me, I felt like I had no free will. I could not speak out and remained without friends during that first year, supposedly an exciting year for any new student abroad. How could they not be utterly scared of this man threatening them? He made sure that his dark secret would not come out and expose him for the monster he really was, while I had to live with minimal contact with the outside world. I am unsure of how long he thought that this strategy would work but it surprisingly did for a very long time.

At the age of 25, I scored a date with a man I had met online, yes that's right, online again. James was very tall, had spiky hair and was a doctor. After giving my father all the details of the time, location and everything I knew about this man, I head out to meet him in a lounge in town. The date went very well, and James and I kissed as people do. Upon returning home, I found Nicolas sitting in the living room in the dark, waiting for me. I could tell that he was angry. He thoroughly questioned me about what exactly I had done with James. I tried to omit the fact that we kissed and so Nicolas kindly informed me that he was sitting in that lounge all along in a dark corner watching us. I was seriously very creeped out by this sentence as now the stalking had reached a new dimension. Nicolas started crying and let me know that if I don't let him touch me that night, I could never see James again. I was 25 years old and a fully working respected professional at that point. This disgusting man abused me that same night and even then, forbid me to ever see James again. I hated my life from morning until evening through the night and repeat.

Writing this sounds unbelievable to me as I reflect back on all of it, so I suspect reading this is even more unbelievable and seemingly impossible to understand how it not only happened but continued for such a long time. However, conditioning a child very early on gives the offender the full control of an adult later on, no matter how educated or mature this child becomes, the scared little girl remains within.

You may remember the drawing of the elephant in the beginning of the chapter. This big, strong elephant is held by a fragile rope. The elephant could easily break free, but it doesn't. Why not?

As a man was passing the elephants, he suddenly stopped, and he was confused as to why these huge animals were being held by a simple thin rope tied to their front leg. There were no chains, and they were not held in a locked cage. The man went up to a trainer close by and asked him why the elephants didn't even try to break free, when they so easily could. The trainer replied: 'When they are very young and much smaller, we use the same size rope to tie them, and at that age, it's enough to hold them. As they grow up, they are conditioned to believe that they can't break away. They believe that the rope can still hold them, so they never even try to break free.'

Like the man passing by wondering why these elephants did not set themselves free with one simple step, many people have asked me why, did I not press charges when I was younger when I must have realised that the abuse was not 'normal' in any way. Like the elephant, I was also conditioned day in, day out, since the age of 9 that I had no power to break free. I was threatened regularly to believe that if this secret came out, that I would be the one punished. The conditioning of the little girl, the fear instilled from a very young age was just as present at 26 like it was at 9.

This strong belief that the abuser had the ultimate power over me which he assured I was reminded of by his omnipresence in my life was enough for me to keep quiet and live on with shame and guilt. It does not surprise me when I hear that survivors have waited 15 years before speaking about the abuse by priests for example. I am always defending them as people who have no idea of what it is like to go through this hell, casually comment: 'Why didn't they say something earlier?'. Unfortunately for Nicolas, I also had the excellent memory of an elephant and could fill pages out at the police station with details, even of the abuse that happened 16 years prior. An elephant never forgets.

At the height of the threats and absolute solid control, I had some very dark thoughts of ending it all as an escape but how glad am I to never have succumbed to those thoughts. I had the stubborn will to live on despite carrying a heavy load within me during the 16 years of silence. If you believe that your life is no longer worthwhile and that you cannot continue, let me tell you that you very well can. You too have the inner strength and determination to see it through. Disappearing from this planet only means that your abuser wins. You will cling on to life because you are worthy and deserving of living a joyful and peaceful life and one day you will report the criminal who has attempted to destroy you and get the justice for yourself and for that little child that lives on within you.

Gradually, Nicolas lost more and more control of his possession over me and became genuinely worried that I may speak out. My sister, Denise who lived with me at the time, was used to reporting my every move to our father on a daily basis. She was his little spy. Even in my apartment, Nicolas would casually lock the door of my bedroom to freely abuse me while Denise was revising in the room next door, not in the slightest bothered by what was happening a few meters away from her.

One night, when I was already sleeping, Nicolas asked Denise to steal my car keys and give them to him. She did that without questioning the morals of such behaviour. He took my car, of which I was still paying back a loan on and changed the ownership over to Elena, another sister, in Luxembourg. A few weeks before, I had gone back home, and Nicolas hid my car keys. I needed to go back to the UK to work and Nicolas made me sign a blank paper, with which he then fabricated a 'contract' on later on, stating that I was apparently selling my car to Elena. On that same visit, he also told Elena and Denise to hide my phone. They obeyed without questioning any demand that he asked of them, like they were programmed robots. Nicolas said he would not give me the car keys or my phone back unless I signed that blank paper. Elena could then easily change the ownership of the car.

I was 26 years old at that time and a fully qualified professional to put things into context. Unbeknown to any of them, I had a copy of my car key with me in the UK. One day, I travelled home and reclaimed my car that the sisters had stolen from me. I drove to the nearest police station to ask how to change the ownership back to my name as I was still paying a loan on that car. My doing this, unnerved Nicolas for probably the first time, as it felt that the scales of control were changing. The sisters had contacted him to tell him that I had taken the car back. He threatened me aggressively on the phone and asked me to do the 'right thing'. The irony of it. He even followed me to the UK to catch me, he wasn't about to stand for what I had done. I was very unsure as to how much harm he would have inflicted upon me if he had physically caught up with me in his sinister rage. I knew he had gone after me, so I fled to Luxembourg. He stormed into my workplace in the UK and demanded to speak to me. Searching for me in the laboratory, I'm so thankful I wasn't there as things escalated from then on.

Back in Luxembourg, I had arrived at the police station. I was asked questions about the car and the police officer called Denise and Elena to the station. They reluctantly came and sat opposite me. It was very tense and uncomfortable between us. With a straight face, Elena said that I had sold the car to her and that I had received the money as per contract. Many people can lie without an ounce of suspicion. She was very practised and good at it. Finally, the officer told me that he was sorry, but I had to give the key back to Elena as it was 'her' car. That was the tipping point that made my glass overflow. The 'car incident' will always be known as the blatant trigger that brought such infuriating injustice to smack me directly in the face, with the culprits sitting right in front of me, lying through their teeth.

With no warning, without planning it in my head beforehand, I snapped. I finally had been pushed to my limit and saw red as the years of torture ran through as visuals in my mind at great speed. No more could I keep this burden to myself, no longer was I prepared to suffer in silence and bear the immense strain. Bursting into anger I began to verbally unravel in detail to the two sisters, who felt like strangers, that sat in front of me, about how their father abused me for 16 years. I mentioned the sordid details that normally would have shocked any person hearing it. The reaction from the sisters after my emotional admission was to smile and there was no sign of any shock or disgust between them. The officer was very surprised at their reaction as it was just inhumane. Their only verbal response to the horrid allegations I had just poured out for the first time in 16 years was for Elena to reveal that 'Papa has done so much for you and you would not professionally be where you are today if it was not for him, you owe him'. Denise confirmed Elena's statement and added that I would have been nothing without him, all said with their smug smiles on their faces.

The police officer heard everything I had said and told me he had a duty to not ignore what I had just let out.

He went out of the room for a few minutes to make copies and left the three of us alone. The two sisters looked at me with a smile, their legs crossed. They casually asked me whether I had bought new shoes. They liked them a lot apparently. Let's put this into context. This is after I had, moments before, burst out with details of the abuse that was not easy to digest. I was crying quite hysterically the whole time, a mix of fear, deep sadness, fury and relief all rolled into a mass of emotion, and all they could say was that my new shoes looked pretty, as though we had been enjoying small talk. Their insensitive and callous reaction is the result of them being prepared for years beforehand by Nicolas, that one day, I would come up with something against him, and since I was 'mentally unstable' like our mother, it was to be considered a total lie.

Their reaction portrayed none of the emotions one would expect, such as shock, disgust, horror or empathy. The officer at one point, got very irritated by my sisters and told them to stop smiling – did they not realise that their sister was suffering, and their smile was absolutely inappropriate. During the encounter, Denise called our father, who asked to speak to the police officer. He asked him exactly what I had said. That man was omnipresent. He was trying very hard to make sure that his 'secret' did not come out, but slowly it was. The closed drawer had just burst out all over the place and now the process had been started.

My car was then handed back to Elena and I stayed behind at the police station. I could not believe that

I had just disclosed for the first time what happened to me since my childhood. It was absolutely surreal, and I felt very disconnected from reality, as in a trance state attempting to make sense of what I had just said out loud. It was as if by verbalising the abuse for the first time in so many years, I was only then realising how grave it was. It was as if it was the first time, I had become conscious of it, right there at the police station. Prior to this encounter, I had never envisioned that this moment could ever become a reality.

Even though I was somehow relieved, I was very scared of what Nicolas would do to me.
A few days later, he stormed into my workplace in Luxembourg and started looking for me as he did in the UK. My employer at the time protected me and let me hide in the basement during the encounter. The following day, I received a message from my family who kindly arranged for a catholic priest Father Marcus from Paris to visit me in order to exorcise me of all the demons that possessed me. They were apparently responsible for all this 'nonsense' I had told the police. I started receiving death threats from my younger brother Leonard, telling me that he was now at a point of no return. From every side, I was threatened and told that I should retract what I had said or else I would regret it.

The day after the 'car incident', I was referred to the main police investigator. I was thoroughly questioned by the police and my teary statements that were conveniently repressed for 16 years were recorded on video. They were harrowing to sit through, but I was now motivated by a sense of seeking justice and of doing what was right. Nicolas was invited to the police station to explain himself. It was my word against his.

I did not have any tangible evidence to prove anything as I had been deleting all the threatening and sexually motivated texts and emails for years as a means of dissociating myself from reality. The recordings were shown to Nicolas. He defended himself, at first by saying that I was a liar and an actress and that nothing I said was true. He then dug his own grave by modifying his testimonies. He started by justifying that in fact, all that he had done had been out of 'medical purpose' because I was unable to take care of myself as opposed to his other daughters. He said that he had to 'help' me because I was 'special'. He tried to convince the investigators that I had misunderstood everything and that what he had done, couldn't possibly be classified as abuse.

His other defence consisted in trying to prove that I inherited the 'crazy genes' from my mother. Out of the six children, apparently, I was the only one burdened with that inheritance, the others were seemingly perfectly sane. I wondered if he actually believed his own lies. During the investigation, I decided to contact Luke again after many years of silence in order to make things straight. He agreed to meet up with me at a restaurant in town. I explained to him that the decision to break up and other numerous events were absolutely out of my control. With a heavy heart, I told him that I had been abused for 16 years and that I now had a police investigation ongoing. Luke did not seem phased by the horrid abuse I was confiding in him. He let me finish what I had to say and then blatantly told me that I should stop lying. My sisters had apparently contacted him shortly after my police complaint to warn him that I am a schizophrenic liar. I tried to fix my conscience towards Luke, but he was not ready for that. I can only hope that he will, one day, read this book and realise that I had no intention of breaking his heart. I was simply a puppet on a string and too ashamed to speak out.

Friends and acquaintances from my childhood, adolescence and adulthood were called in to testify. Former female friends came forward and made allegations against Nicolas that dated back to our adolescence. I had no idea about those at the time. Family members were called in to testify. I am somehow glad to have had so many siblings that contradicted each other on many occasions, muddying all that was being portrayed by their version of events, so the truth was quite clear. I did not need to put in too much effort to prove that I was not lying. The truth will always prevail. The memories of such abuse will always remain despite being locked away in a drawer in the back of my mind. Regardless of how long ago the abuse happened, the memories remain vivid and my answers were always the same as all I had to do was to recall them each time I was questioned. I have learnt to cope with the memories by creating distance around them and now I have a third person perspective on the events themselves. Today, I can talk about the happenings with full emotional dissociation. It is as if I was talking about another person to whom this has happened. I learnt to have a pragmatic approach after the trial.

Shortly after filing the complaint, Nicolas was arrested and held in prison for two years without trial. His statements were very contradictory, and I was believed. The threats continued and Denise wrote a letter to the investigator saying that they should immediately release Nicolas as he is God sent and that she would die for him. When I saw that letter, the clear resemblance to some sort of a cult was very apparent to me. During his detention, Andreas made sure that his father's case landed in the media. Nicolas went on a hunger strike to protest about being held captive without trial and Andreas made enough noise to get him into the newspapers.

Over the course of the investigations, I had to undergo numerous psychological tests to prove that I was not making up stories. The tests concluded that I was indeed not mentally unstable nor showed any reason to invent such grave allegations against my own procreator. Nicolas also underwent psychological tests. It turned out that he did not have the typical paedophile profile. He was 'diagnosed' as an opportunistic sexual predator. He found an opportunity and slowly began the process of his grooming. I don't know how much of it was planned and conscious and how much was improvised.

I naturally asked my therapist at the time, why I had waited until the age of 26 to speak out. She answered that I had seen how he could imprison my mother in a psychiatric facility for months on end, so I was naturally afraid of that. She also said that if I had said something when I was 15 for example, it was my word against an adult's, and he would most likely have sent me on the basis of the 'schizophrenia inheritance' to join my mother. She reminded me that at 15, I had no support, no money, no degree and that 10 years prior, the topic of abuse was still taboo and not taken as seriously as it was when I pressed charges. I obviously never planned to burst in a police station with horrid details of the abuse in front of my two sisters but subconsciously I assume that all these factors must have played a role in giving me the courage to dare to finally speak out.

While being held behind bars, Nicolas tried his best to ruin my professional reputation by sending out long handwritten letters to each formal institution that I had a link with, to depict me as unfit for practice, mentally unstable and a liar. In his 15 page long psychopathic letters, he accused me of being a drug addict, a sexual predator and a cheater. I was apparently performing fraudulent laboratory experiments, being unfit to care for patients and I was seemingly turning up to work after dancing all night in clubs without prior sleep. My sisters Denise and Elena did not hesitate one moment to personally hand in these letters to the institutions in Luxembourg, with full knowledge of what our father was depicting me as in these pages. I struggled to understand how they could do so, with full consciousness against their very own sister. I concluded that this was their way of 'revenge' for a childhood filled with extreme jealousy towards me.

The judge at the time made Nicolas write a follow up letter to each of these institutions apologising and retracting every word that he had said about me. I felt I was being heard by the authorities, which was validating for me, while being under attack by my own family. They could not believe what I was accusing the 'good man' of and they chose not to believe it as that would make them accomplices. All my family are highly educated, yet education has got nothing to do with moral values. If you choose to blindly accept something that is fundamentally wrong and blatantly obvious, and do not take any steps to prevent it from happening, you become an accomplice - no matter how well educated you are. I even received telephone calls from my own mother and grandmother telling me to 'confess in church for what I had done to my father'. Needless to say, I hung up and have not felt the need to speak to them since. It is hard to begin to comprehend this behaviour, especially when it's coming from your own family.

I completely dissociated myself from my family, for my own sanity and self-worth. Blood turns out to be not as thick as I thought or what society conditions us to believe. The siblings finally showed their real selves and would have done anything to protect their father from being punished for what he had done to me. Their loyalty was clear. They went to great lengths in order to break me. They finally received the approval from their father that they desperately longed for during their childhood, adolescence and adult life. They were notably worth more than the favourite child and felt righteous in acting against me, fuelled by their hidden jealousy which stemmed from their childhood.

There was very obvious favouritism in my family, which produced anger and envy towards me, accumulated and provoked by Nicolas' behaviours. This reaction included both my own mother and the rest of the family. The four years of investigations and trials revealed their suppressed feelings, which made them act against me in order to protect our father, regardless of any moral principles. The siblings always felt 'less' than me and they had the urge to follow the same career path as mine in order to show their father that they were as 'good' as the 'perfect Mary'.

After four drawn out and intense years of criminal investigations and trials, that received a great deal of media attention, Nicolas was finally sentenced to 15 years in prison. The day I saw him being escorted in handcuffs and locked into the police van was undoubtedly the best day of my life. Some justice had been served and for me, that allowed for some healing. Within these same four years of trials, I continued working, got married, gave birth to my first two children and wrote and defended my PhD thesis. I believe that my sheer determination to see some justice and the love for my children kept me going. Heavily pregnant, I was attacked and humiliated by the adverse party in front of the judges, not only by the defence lawyer but by the people that should have been protecting me, my own family. Shockingly, they lied over and over again, under oath, in order to protect the offender. I was depicted as a lying, mentally unstable, money seeking individual, that according to the defence 'could in no way be a victim of sexual abuse, considering the successful career path taken'. Appearances can be deceptive.

Seeing Nicolas being shouted at by the judge during the trial made me feel sorry for him. That pity was coming from the unhealthy foundations that my parents gave to me. It was as if you can hurt me as much as you want, but I will always be a good person and have empathy for you. This had to change. I had to remind myself that this man sitting there like a beaten-up dog had stolen 16 years of my life and beyond. My lawyer reminded me of the horrific abuse he put me through. She had to show me my own handwritten testimonies so that it was visual for me as I had nobody to protect me at that point. Nobody was there to remind me of my self-worth when I needed it the most. Being heavily pregnant during the trial also didn't help my distorted empathy for the offender.

During the first year of my doctorate, I had met a man, again through an online platform and also based in Luxembourg while I was in the UK. I may need to point out that for as long as I can remember, our father made us believe that the only partner that we could possibly marry would need to be of Luxembourgish origin. Let me elaborate on that.

During my first year at university, a dark-skinned student Edward was fancying me. When Nicolas received a diverted text message from that young man to his phone, revealing his crush on me, he did not hesitate to call him personally. He carried on stating that 'Mary would never date a black man; how could he even believe that he had a chance with her. Mary was too good for him, the only person she would be dating would be from a pure white Luxembourgish family'. I listened to all of this in embarrassment from afar and needless to say that Edward despised me after that racist phone call. I unconsciously followed that instruction and the only way of finding a Luxembourger when one is overseas was definitely not in a British pub.

Felix is tall, slim and has straight teeth. He likes fast cars, dehydrated pasta and has no affinity for fruit or vegetables. On the first date, I was obliged to take Mira along as per my father's orders. She was meant to watch me so that she could report back to Nicolas. I was 25 years old at the time. She was very bored being the third wheel and sat the whole night in a corner in the nightclub. Felix was not the romantic type. He did not drown me in compliments or presents to show his love to me like Luke did. Somehow, his kindness and pragmatism appealed to me and it did not take long before I got into a relationship with him. I thought I found in him a good man whom I could trust. I had finally found my soulmate in my newly found freedom, so I thought. Our sense of humour was matching, which, for me seemed to be a number one requirement in a partner. As the French saying goes, 'femme qui rit, à moitié dans ton lit' rings very true with me.

Felix was in Sweden when I gave the police declaration. I had nobody in Luxembourg to support me as I had been away in the UK for a decade and had lost links with old friends. Felix' family treated me well and I felt like I could be myself. The relief was enormous and finally, I could breathe and endured the four difficult years that followed my courageous report at the police station. Felix never influenced my decision to file the complaint, he was not in the country. It was driven by the deep feeling of injustice about my car that constituted the last drop. It was never about a car, but the car was the trigger that made me realise that the sisters, who sat in front of me were not really my sisters.

Felix and his family gave me the safe haven that I never had before then. I was now surrounded by a real family that seemed genuine and supportive. They listened to me and seemed very protective over me. It felt good to feel that someone was there to defend me against evil. It felt right. Even though in this case, the evil were the very people that were meant to protect me. I finally was not alone in this and could count on a family to keep me safe. I could now move on to the next life chapter with Felix, leaving everything behind.

How I survived this ordeal for 16 years followed by four difficult years of trial is still a conundrum to me as I reflect back now. I recognised the power of a smile very early on. How could the abuse go unnoticed for so many years if I hadn't sent my brain a message that declared 'everything is fine' when it was not at all the case. It could all have turned out very differently, but the will to survive is within each of us. Often, we don't realise just the incredible strength we possess until it is tested. And tested it certainly was, every single day. No matter how difficult the issue may seem today that you may be experiencing, you too can find your survival instinct. Have no doubt that it exists. My strategy that helped me to cope from the daily abuse and the toxic environment that I was trapped in, was to dive into my academic books and temporarily lose myself in them. This served me well in the end.

There can be many reasons why you feel like you are not ready to take that first step and report your abuser. Perhaps you fear that you will not be believed and that the case will be dismissed due to insufficient evidence? Maybe the abuse happened too long ago to be 'eligible' for reporting? Perhaps you fear the repercussions that this outing may have on your life? Perhaps the abuser has full power over you, and you still feel that you are incapable of denouncing him because he is 'stronger'? I understand. Let me remind you that you have all of the strength within you, you may need to dig deep but please report that criminal today. Hold onto the faith that you will get through this, only YOU are able to take that step, nobody can do it for you.

You will be intensely questioned, so be prepared. You will need to open up tightly closed drawers in your mind that have been conveniently shut for many years. You may have to disclose very private and secretive details of the abuse you have suffered. You will be humiliated and depicted as a liar during the investigations and trials. You will have feelings of shame bubbling up inside of you and you may perhaps have some regret rear its ugly head as you go that extra step in reporting your abuser. Let me tell you first-hand, that even if, appeal after appeal, the judges conclude that the case is dismissed because of lack of evidence, you will feel freedom and inner peace. It will be out in the open and despite having to see your criminal freely walking around, you will have done it for you, you broke the silence, and you will live on with your head held up high with pride. Nothing can take that away from you and it is the greatest gift that is available for you.

Even if the case is dismissed, which could be devastating to you, the criminal didn't win. The power is in your hands. The abuser can only win by you holding yourself imprisoned in your own body and mind, keeping that 'secret' to yourself. The offender really has no power over you, even though it may feel like it. Like me, you may lose your family after such an outing and you may realise that blood relationships really mean nothing to you, but you will get through this. You are not alone. People all over the world are silently keeping their secrets too - you will find your support network even if it means dismissing your own family after they have shown their true colours. In my case, the offender received a long prison sentence, and I came out of this stronger than ever, even if it meant living on without any family. I stood for what was right and I was willing to accept the consequences, whatever the repercussions may have been. I am very proud to have broken the silence and to have rebounded as a survivor encouraging others to speak up.

Regardless of the nature of the abuse, you are stronger than you give yourself credit for. I am not unique nor special, you too can do it and get through this. Remind yourself of what you have lived through already and how, once upon a time, that would have seemed impossible. It is in your power to get away from that 'victim' stamp on your forehead and embrace the 'survivor' stamp. That stamp will most likely never disappear and rightly so. That stamp is the scar of your battle.

During the trial, I was desperately looking for groups of people who had been going through a similar trauma that I could identify myself with. There was nothing at all on offer at the time that I could find. I longed to talk to like-minded people and learn about coping strategies. Talking to friends was simply not enough for me at the time. My friends had compassion and love for me but the deeper understanding and empathy from having been through what I had been through, was missing. I started buying every book that was related to sexual abuse. I couldn't get enough of the information and personal stories and soon realised that my story was not that atypical. I was frantically searching for answers. A similar reaction I found which was common, was the family rejecting the victim and protecting the offender. It was not surprising. It stands to reason that if the family started to accept the victim's allegations as truth, it would undermine the foundation of the family and where would that leave everyone? It's then far easier to close one's eyes to the reality and pretend that everything is just fine when in fact, it is crumbling. It is easier to reject one person than rejecting the idea of the perfect family. It is easier to say that a person is mentally unstable and a liar, than to face the reality that the almighty patriarch has caused this much pain. Who would want to face up to agonising truths such as these?

Eleven years on, following my declaration to the police, I still question how my family is able to live on with a pure conscience after hurting and abandoning me. I often wonder how they quietly continue to be happy with this heavy guilt as if nothing ever happened. Is there even guilt when one does not acknowledge the truth? I have come to the conclusion that feelings of guilt are very subjective and that this feeling can't exist if the moral values are not in the right place to begin with. This relinquishes the person of any responsibility. I will never have the answers to the questions I still have for my family and I have made peace with this. I am not mourning the loss of a family anymore. I believe the values as such, the true foundations were never there in the first place, as sad as that might be to read.

Following the trial, I began to deeply analyse how a whole family can turn against one person for speaking up about such a grave behaviour by a victim's very own father. I quickly realised that despite most families being dysfunctional to a certain degree, my specific family was very cult-like. It consisted of a group of people living under one roof, each to their own. Heading the troop was a very controlling and charismatic leader who, up to this day, gives instructions to his children, despite them being adults. They would die for this man. They worship him and blindly follow his commands as they openly showed during the investigations.

During the first few years, Nicolas justified his presence in prison to everyone who was willing to hear it. He used to say he was put there by God to guide the other prisoners onto the right moral path. It was not because he had done anything wrong, but he had a humanity mission to accomplish. It is interesting to observe how one person can manipulate this many people to this extent. Cults are indeed interesting to study as they need specific conditions to thrive. A charismatic, persuasive, powerful leader is worshipped by his followers without questioning his truths and beliefs. He is fully in control of their thinking and their actions. They blindly follow his orders without ever doubting the righteousness of their actions. There is a true conviction firmly held by the followers that the leader is always right and is somehow God sent.

The reactions of the family to my allegations were very surprising as there was absolutely no shock or disbelief demonstrated by them. After my first declaration, Andreas played a double game in that he pretended to be 'on my side' for about a year. At the time, I was pleased and relieved to have at least someone believe me and question the intentions and actions of our father. Little did I know however, was that Andreas was taking each information that I volunteered, straight to Nicolas in prison. Andreas finally found the approval from his father that he had been longing for, for decades. Since childhood, Andreas was rarely appreciated by his father, whom he immensely admired. Why Nicolas chose to name his firstborn son after a globally hated dictator, linked to the most horrible atrocities known to mankind, will never cease to amaze me. I shall mention that my older brother's real first name is not Andreas.

Playing his double game allowed Andreas to finally receive the prestigious pat on the back that he had desperately yearned for despite all of the physical and emotional pain that his father inflicted upon him. Interestingly, Andreas had changed his original testimony in which he depicted his father as a controlling narcissist and tyrant while he was supposedly 'on my side'. Later on, he went back to the investigator to retract his first statement to be replaced by one in which he described the father as very caring and loving, then allowed his suppressed jealousy to flood out freely in his declarations. The credibility of these statements had obviously been doubted as their truth was constantly contradicted. During secondary school, Andreas and I not only attended the same school, but we were also put in the same class. I was the best student, whereas he was the worst and comparisons were constantly made by the teachers. I can only guess how much this contributed to Andreas' bottled-up jealousy against me over the years in addition to seeing me being 'preferred' by our father at home.

A couple of years ago, Nicolas was prematurely released from prison. I was told that he was becoming expensive on the taxpayer. He was being isolated from the other inmates as there apparently exists a hierarchy in prison, in which paedophiles and rapists come last, and often get assaulted by the criminals who serve a sentence for theft or for afflicting bodily harm. Nicolas also tried to simulate a brain tumour at some point in order to win a few points, rouse sympathy and get an early release. His brother, who is a surgeon in the US, certified that due to his old age and his apparent brain tumour, he should be released early. Andreas is a film producer and reserved special roles for Nicolas in his movies following his early release. Nothing had changed, Andreas was still hopelessly looking to please the man that had hurt him physically and indirectly damaged his self-confidence.

Since my childhood, my mother treated me differently to my other siblings. It felt like she considered me as a rival and someone to compete with for the attention of her husband, and not as her daughter. She confirmed that in her statements when she was questioned during the investigations. She used to hug the other five siblings and willingly give them affection while not even talking to me. I have grown up with the feeling of being resented by my own mother. She had no love for me and made that very apparent. Like the siblings, she also displayed suppressed jealousy towards me in her witness testimonies. She had let her husband fully take advantage of her daughter and it was very obvious. She did nothing to protect me from harm as a loving mother would normally do. She contributed to the abuse by closing her eyes to what was happening for years, not even looking out for me behind locked doors. After having my own children, I can't even start to comprehend how a mother could do such things. This has only served to give me more willingness to protect my children. Understandably, I have more vigilance about this topic when it comes to my own children.

As my children grew older, they started to question which tummy I came out of? Did I also have parents like Felix did? What do they look like? Where do they live? What's my mother's name? What colour is her house? At the time, I couldn't answer anything other than 'Mummy's parents were not nice to mummy, and that's why mummy doesn't want to see them'. I knew that, as my children grow, their questions will undoubtedly grow to be more specific. I attended a few seminars in which I tried to learn how best to approach this sensitive topic with my children. It was a mix of wanting to fiercely protect them and being open enough to educate them.

I still haven't figured out how to correctly handle this topic with them. Books like *I said No!* by Kimberly King, help me speak to my children with a visual aid. As parents, we keep telling our children not to speak to anyone they don't know and not to accept any present from anyone who's not familiar to them. What about the people that they know? Let's not forget that in most cases, sexual abuse does not happen in a white van by a stranger. The concept is pretty successful because of the abuse happening in the close circle of the child by someone they trust. If the child is not abused by their parent, it can be by the uncle, aunt, cousin, sibling, priest, teacher, friend, grandfather, grandmother, family friend, neighbour and the list goes on. Sexual abuse has no limits of gender or age. It is rarely a person that the child has never seen before. Kimberly's book carefully highlights the red flags but also the green flags. One should not start scaring the child and making them feel that the world is a very unsafe place. Using the right terms in the right tone goes a long way.

After Nicolas was finally convicted, I felt a strong urge to go out into primary and secondary schools and talk to the pupils about that taboo subject that many prefer to brush under the carpet and hide away like a dirty, shameful secret. I asked my psychologist at the time, why this wasn't an open subject that was discussed in schools. Her answer was simply that talking about this to children would probably reveal many abuse cases and the country lacked the resources to deal with the potential outings. That was very baffling to me. I will always wonder if a psychologist, other professional or a survivor had come to my school and sat us down to say that 'if a parent/aunt/uncle/grandparent touches you in that area, it is absolutely not OK', I may have had an insight on what was wrong and what was not. This is the starting point, having the awareness and knowledge to rely on that something is wrong, because abused children are brainwashed into believing the sexual acts are normal and to keep quiet about it. We need to do more to protect our children. No child should have to endure what I endured. I am determined to change the whole landscape and bring justice in whatever way I can.

Since my children were used to seeing childhood photos of Felix at their grandparents' house, they asked their grandmother if she had pictures of me as a baby. I then realised that I did not have a single picture of myself as a child which saddened me, and it prompted me to contact the probation officer of Nicolas. I demanded to have the childhood photos that Nicolas had of me. I received a bag full of old photos and surprisingly, a letter from my mother asking to meet me and my children. I threw the letter away. This meeting will most likely never take place. I sat down on the floor with my children one evening and we started going through the old family photos. I let my children cut my face out of them. The other unwanted faces went straight to the bin. That felt very empowering. I then made a collage with the few faces I had of myself as a baby and a toddler and this remains the only family that my children will ever know from my side.

Chapter Three

*I'm not upset that you lied to me,
I'm upset that from now on I can't believe you.*
Friedrich Nietzsche

It was too good to be true.

Years later, the walls are still white and cold. Waiting on our turn in that same tribunal building, I feel very defeated. I see him sitting on the opposite side of the room, laughing confidently with his lawyer. I can feel my baby kick in response to the adrenaline rushing through my veins while tears are flowing down my exhausted face.

The storm had settled, and life was finally going in the right direction for me. I felt like I had found a substitute family that loved me unconditionally, a safe base. I even enjoyed the imposed weekly Sunday lunches at my mother in law's house. Being in her home made me feel like nothing bad could happen to me while being surrounded by a family that seemed to care for me. I was very attracted to Felix and his laid-back manner. Like me, he was not the type of person that easily got nervous and had the ability to tackle issues with pragmatism. This is what I needed at this point as the storm had been very emotional. I was convinced that Felix was the man I wanted to spend the rest of my life with. I was so sure that I took all my courage and publicly asked him to marry me. I had asked the cinema if they could put my marriage proposal on screen after the movie and they found the idea original. The day had come, and I was very nervous to say the least. What if he says no? What if he storms out of the cinema? I did not know how Felix would react to my public declaration of love.

After watching a romantic comedy starring Jennifer Aniston, the moment had come. A romantic poem appeared on the screen with a love song entitled *After tonight* by Justin Nozuka, playing in the background. I looked over at Felix and he was not paying attention to the screen so I remained on my seat, hoping he would look up and see 'Will you marry Mary?' displayed in huge format and he finally did. My heart was racing, I was not sure what was going through his mind. He did not say a word and timidly smiled. I did not know what to expect. He was finally asked by the cinema manager whether it's a 'yes or no' and Felix replied 'yes'. I was relieved and the photographer of the cinema took a photo of us that appeared in the newspaper. Felix kept that newspaper article for years in his wallet. Felix was not particularly touched by my public love declaration. I accepted it and put it down to his introverted nature.

Felix' mother Melanie treated me like the daughter she never had. Melanie is tanned, displays a short hairdo and likes to eat her food very fast. She rarely smiles even when she is happy. She took me shopping for a wedding dress. I enjoyed being taken care of, a feeling

I never had the chance to experience. Melanie spoilt me with delicious cooking, she made sure I felt safe in her family. She took me to salt caves to relax and talked to me for hours in order to make sense of what had happened to me over the past decades. It was in a way therapeutic, yet it felt intrusive at the same time. I could not shake off the feeling that her curiosity to know more details about the abuse was prevailing over her motherly care for me.

Melanie even took me to a fortune teller. Upon arrival at her house, the lady did not resemble the image that I had of a clairvoyant. She was a regular woman living in a regular yellow house in a regular neighborhood. With a simple look and feel of the palm of my hand, she proceeded to tell me that my future looked amazing. According to her, my past was very turbulent and from now on my life would be a smooth, joyful ride. I pretended to be impressed by all that she knew about me, pretending not to know that Melanie had obviously briefed her prior to the meeting.

My wedding day was set. I was very excited about being married and finally building my own family. It was empowering to stand tall with my soon to be husband after all the turbulence. Back then, I often dreamed at work, imagined living with my husband in a big house with our children happily running around in a big garden. That vision was beautiful in my eyes. Felix and I had decided that we would only have a small wedding. That was fine by me as I was not the type of person that enjoyed being in the spotlight. I did not fancy having eyes on me. My shy nature was not at ease with being the centre of attention. After years of trials that exposed me, I understandably welcomed being invisible. On my special day, I felt like a beautiful bride. One of the rare occasions that I truly found myself pretty. The dress perfectly fitted my slim figure, my hair was made up and the make-up was natural, yet perfect for me. It was an amazing day despite me having no family attending and most guests being from Felix' family and friends.

Many years after the storm had slipped into a distant memory, it felt like no matter how much I proved to Felix' family that I was just 'normal', I would never get away from the status of being a 'victim' in their eyes. I would always feel like the little girl that was 'saved' by Felix and his family. Often, my story became the main topic of casual dinner conversations initiated by Melanie to her friends while I was sat there and had no voice. At some point, the life of Felix' parents seemed to revolve around my story. It really felt like it gave these average pensioners a purpose in life, adding some sensation to their otherwise rather uneventful retirement. They felt like they had saved me from evil.

For four years, no matter what I did to show that I was a survivor and not in any way impacted by my past, I was defined by the 'victim' stamp on my forehead. That status never shifted as I realised years later. The abuse is a big part of my life, but it has never defined me. I functioned very well, held down a full-time career, did my best to be a good wife to my husband

and a loving mother to my children. Surprisingly, I was prepared to accept that 'victim' stamp for years in return for the new caring family I was given. Perhaps, I compromised my own self-respect and let Melanie and her family feel like they had truly contributed to my successful trial, so that they could feel good about themselves? Perhaps, I had no energy left to defend myself and casually accepted any treatment as long as it remotely resembled care and love. At some point, I must have assumed that any attention was better than no attention at all.

Life seemed just right, and I felt like, finally the wheel had turned in my favour. I came out of this trial victorious to have been heard and believed. It was incredibly healing. I felt secure with my new family and could finally turn the page to a new beginning. I found great satisfaction in a new job and life was stressful yet fulfilling. I gave up my evenings, weekends and holidays for my career. I was always accessible and ready to sort out any issue that came up immediately. I received great acknowledgment and felt like my work was worthwhile. I soon realised after coming back from maternity leave that everyone is replaceable, no matter how good you think you are at your job. There will always be someone that can take over your role. Even though it is hard to accept it, we are all disposable. You could be at the height of your career today and God forbid you become ill, have a child or are forced to take a few months out of your job for any other reason, you may realise that you are not special in any way. Your employer is likely to only appreciate your work in the present moment and will not hesitate to replace you at any time if necessary, easily forgetting all of the prior commitment you have shown.

My sincere advice is not to sacrifice your everything to any job or employer, no matter how 'important' you may feel at work. It may all be over sooner than you think. You will not get that lost time back. Your children will grow up and only remember you sitting at a laptop or staring at a phone. Look them in the eyes, cuddle and play with them TODAY, it may all be too late tomorrow. Put aside any distracting devices, work can wait until tomorrow. Live in the present and enjoy these precious moments with your children, create memories, it's now or never.

Strangely enough, during that same job, only one year on after the end of the trial, Denise and Leonard were also employed at the same research institute and during the following years, I saw them day in, day out. It was a daily painful reminder of the fact that they had let me down and yet life continued as though nothing had happened. A few people at work knew that we were siblings because I had mentioned it. Finally, one day, after over three years of working with them, I summoned up all of my courage and addressed them. I asked them outright all of the questions that still plagued my heart. I quickly realised that both were still the same people that had lied under oath against me a few years earlier. Their maturity had not progressed any further. I realised there was absolutely no need to waste any energy or time on anyone. One can't change people. It was not my goal and I learnt that I must readily let go as there was no added value for me at all. Justice will never be fully made, and I must accept that. I needed to come to terms with that chapter of my life and move on.

Likewise, I also came across Elena numerous times as she was employed at the pharmacy near my children's paediatrician. She has, therefore seen my children on many occasions when she took our prescription. It is somehow strange that she could see her nephews knowing that she will never be allowed contact with them. The last I have heard of Mira, is that she's moved to Japan. God knows what career she's pursuing in Tokyo; I suspect a modelling one.

When I was young, I never thought about getting married and having children. I was not the type of girl that pictured herself in a wedding dress and I rarely played with a baby doll, pretending to be her mother. A year into my marriage, I started to notice more and more children around. The pure innocence of a child was simply beautiful to observe. That carefree happiness, that funny clumsiness and this unconditional love for their parents intrigued me. It was as if I never had the chance to experience this carefree childhood and I somehow wanted to relive it through my own children. At the age of 28, I started to have a deep longing to start my own family. I was tearing up whenever I saw a baby around, it was very emotional, as if I felt incomplete. Perhaps indirectly, I was looking to build my own blood related family since mine was absent in my life. I was lucky enough to easily fall pregnant and eight months later, I was holding my beautiful firstborn in my arms. He was so perfect that 18 months later, I was cradling my next born.

Parenting came very natural to me and I rarely felt overwhelmed. Felix was also in his element and he was enjoying raising our children with me. A few years later, we welcomed another bundle of love. Having a third baby did not seem to add more stress to everyday life. The only noticeable change was the extra laundry and the need for a bigger car. We thoroughly found pleasure watching our small family grow bigger. The love between the siblings and the affection that the children gave us was something I had not known before then and I was determined to protect and love our children no matter what.

A few years had passed, and my world came crashing down all over again when I had to bury my stillborn daughter just two weeks after my 34th birthday. My body thought that a baby was in my arms and reacted in response. It produced milk and I experienced strong uterine contractions when in fact that baby was no longer. The heartbreak I felt was indescribable. I had shown extreme resilience to life's hits prior to that, however, that birth, yet death, totally broke me emotionally. I was consumed with immense guilt, feelings that I were to blame, and the death of my baby haunted me. Everyone around me went about their usual business while I was suffering in a way that I never thought possible up until then. I developed a bout of extreme insomnia and tried to deal with the insurmountable and perpetual grief in my own way. One day, I had the urge to do something that I believed may relieve that pain and I had my baby girl's real footprints tattooed on the back of my arm. This way, she is always with me and it somehow felt good experiencing the pain of the needle while creating that artwork on my body.

I promised my daughter that I will honour her existence the same way that I acknowledge my other wonderful children. She is as precious to me as my other children are. Today, when my children talk about their siblings, they never omit her. They are growing up with a sister even if she isn't physically present. On many occasions, I overheard how they tell their friends about her. She will always be included in my family and I can't possibly say that I only have four children when I am asked. I have five in total. Each year on her birthday, I take the children to visit her grave and we sing her happy birthday. It has become a family tradition and it makes me smile when I witness the special love that they show her. They greet her with love declarations when we drive by the cemetery. She is alive in our hearts forever.

With the months passing by, life slowly returned to normal. I could soundly sleep, and life was joyful again. The longing for another baby was very strong. This time even more from Felix' side than it was from mine. It was as if the loss of our baby strengthened his desire to grow our family by one more. Following a surgery removing both a suspicious mass and a fallopian tube, I received the wonderful news on my daughter's first anniversary that I was expecting again. I was scared but also felt very grateful to be able to carry another baby. The pregnancy went very well, I blossomed, and I felt like I had it all. I had my job, the husband, the house with a lovely garden and my beautiful children surrounding me. I had created my own family since the one I was given at birth turned out to be traitorous. I was safe in my substitute family. The parents, brothers, aunts, sisters-in-law of Felix all showed support, kindness and care for me. I felt at ease with these people and I had no doubt that if I had any issues of any sort, that they would back me up and support me as a family would do.

The pregnancy progressed and I had reached the eighth month of pregnancy. We were very excited to welcome another sweet baby at home, the children couldn't wait for the birth. They were very impatient, they wanted to finally see him after he kept kicking them through the big belly. They wanted to hold him and already assigned the different roles to each other. One would be responsible for the bath, the other for the bottle and the one that did not have a say, would be assigned the nappy change.

One evening, after putting the children to bed, Felix came up to me and talked to me about an article he had read. He mentioned that it was about a practice called 'polyamory'. He went on to explain that in fact, a person could love many people at the same time and still be committed in a marriage. I was very confused. I did not know why he was bringing this up, so I let him finish. Felix continued and in a seemingly nervous tone asked me if I was interested in such a polyamorous relationship. I was shocked. I thought I had misheard him. Did he really just suggest to me that I date other men while he dates other women? Did he really insinuate that he would not be jealous if I had a relationship with another man and truly believed that I would be fine with him dating another woman after nearly 10 years of marriage? I was very speechless at this point and could only tear up. I was heavily pregnant, and my hormones were racing. At first, I thought that he was joking so I replied that there was no way any man would date me with a watermelon under my shirt. In fact, he was not joking at all. He was serious.

When I realised that he was not kidding, I told him that of course, I would be very jealous, how could he even believe otherwise, I loved him after all. I held back more tears from flowing and left to go to bed. I have never been jealous as Felix never gave me a reason to doubt his faithfulness. I always told people that I was lucky that Felix is the type of man who likes cars and does not look at other women.

That night in bed, crying my eyes out, I was shocked and confused about what Felix had just told me in the living room. I had no idea what to do with this information. Did he even love me? Why would he even suggest dating other women? Was he this unhappy in our marriage? My mind went in every direction and I could not sleep at all, imagining Felix kissing another woman. My heart was racing, I could not calm myself down, I was heartbroken by Felix even thinking about it. I was heartbroken by a simple outspoken intention, not even an actual act. I could not believe how I'd feel if he really touched someone else if I was already this upset by him saying something like this out loud to me. I messaged my best friend Hild in the UK and let her know what Felix had just told me. She was just as shocked, and we concluded that perhaps he was going through a midlife crisis and tomorrow would be a better day.

I could not let this go and I started to really worry that Felix would be thinking of dating someone else. I wrote Felix a very long love letter in which I reiterated my love for him after nearly ten years of marriage. I explained to him how upset I was at the mere thought of him touching someone else. I was convinced at this point that he had never even looked at another woman and what he had proposed the previous night was stemming from a midlife crisis. I saw this as a wakeup call and suggested to him couple therapy and repeated to him that the simple imagination of him being with someone else was enough to break my heart. I suggested we renewed our vows and this time with another beautiful wedding ten years on with our children nicely dressed up. That wedding would be even more meaningful then with the fruit of our love dressed up in white. I could not stop crying since he had proposed that polyamory and with my racing imagination of Felix dating other women, the sleepless, hyperventilating nights began. The few weeks before giving birth were supposed to be dedicated to nesting. I should have been preparing for the arrival of my sweet baby, sleeping peacefully to gather energy before birth and for the sleepless post-partum phase awaiting me. Instead, I was incredibly upset and very distressed about my husband thinking of dating other women.

Felix and I had a long talk after he had read my letter and he reassured me that what he had proposed was just a thought and nothing concrete. He guaranteed that he would never ever touch another woman, he was a married man after all. He gave me the peace of mind that I should not worry and that he loved me as before, nothing had changed. I even agreed to couple therapy to strengthen our relationship. I believed that this was the end of it and that I could now put this behind us and give all my focus back to our baby. I excused Felix by saying this was all part of his midlife crisis, that he was approaching the dreaded 40 and that this was his way of analysing what he may have missed out on in life.

It was a Saturday afternoon and I had just put my 2-year-old to bed for his nap. I then casually went onto Felix' computer in order to see my baby's 4D ultrasound scans as my laptop could not read the disk, very excited to see his growing little body. A pop-up message appeared on Felix' computer screen as I switched it on, from a woman called Anita. I had never heard Felix mention that name before. When I opened the message up, it became very clear from the words in front of me that Felix was having a love affair with Anita. Felix was romantically declaring his love to this woman in a way that he had never talked to me in all these years. He also let her know that he had a great time with her the previous night. In that split second, my heart was broken in a million pieces. My hormones raced into overdrive, adrenaline was flooding into my system and I hyperventilated. It was very surreal. I did not know what to do with myself and whom to talk to about this. I was very confused and distressed about what I had just read. I let Felix know that I had discovered the message by chance and that he should explain himself. He feigned ignorance and made out to not understand what I was talking about. I sent him a photo of the message on the screen, perhaps that would jog his memory, I thought.

One hour after the discovery, I invited Felix' parents to our home in order to see what they thought about the message that I had just seen on their son's screen. They immediately came and so did Felix. With tears flowing down my face, I confronted Felix in front of his parents. He remained silent, put a pillow in front of his face as if he was ashamed about what I had just discovered about him. I started firing questions at him as if in urgent need of details of the adultery. I increasingly raised my voice as I was quite hysterical at this point, thereby waking up my toddler from his nap. Melanie walked up to me and the only reaction she had to this scene was to tell me that I should be 'gentle' on her son as he could 'hurt himself' if I was too harsh with my questions. What about the heavily pregnant woman standing in front of her carrying her grandchild? Did she not care about me hurting myself after that discovery? That statement was enough for me to understand who was going to be the 'victim' here and who was going to have a hard time finding support.

At the time, I did not know the extent of the infidelity. Were we talking about one innocent kiss or more? Were we talking about a one off or had something been going on for months, possibly years? All I felt in my heavily pregnant state was deep sadness, rage and heartbreak. I no longer recognised the man I had married ten years prior to this. Could I really be this wrong in my judgement of people? Still very confused I let Felix explain himself with as much detail as he was willing to give me. I needed to hear it all. After my past, I could not tolerate any more lies and deception. I needed to understand what was wrong with ME. I needed clarification on how a married, seemingly happy father could lead such a double life. I felt that I must be at fault and questioned myself. Was I not pretty enough? Had I birthed too many babies and my body wasn't as fit as a 25-year-old? Was I not adventurous enough in bed? I needed to understand how an adult responsible for four children could selfishly put his family's stability on the line for his own desires. Did he not think that his affair would come out sooner or later and potentially have devastating effects on five other people?

It was very clear that I could never trust this man again. He broke my heart along with my trust, the foundation of our marriage was no more. He did not ask for my consent to be in a polygamous relationship. He misused my trust and put my health and that of my unborn babies in danger by sleeping in parallel for years. At the time, I didn't know that this man, whom I told everyone 'how lucky I was to have found him', was cheating on me for several years. My therapist at the time made sense of my feelings by reminding me that the reason I felt so deeply violated was because Felix did not have my consent to be in a polygamous relationship with me. I felt used and fooled and these feelings were even stronger in my case due to the Deja vu I had with the abuse, where I gave no consent and was freely taken advantage of.

Since the discovery of the affair, Anita kept contacting me in order to see whether I planned on forgiving Felix so that she would know where she stood with him. Both of them let me know that they were in love with each other, but they would be willing to dissolve their relationship if I was willing to take Felix back. I was utterly disgusted and honestly could not comprehend what was going on. Many weeks following the discovery, Anita even contacted me to complain about her poor judgement in men and that she always gets hurt. Me, being the kind Mary put all my pain aside and offered her free counselling sessions on her love life. How stupid of me when I reflect back. This only goes to show that my self-respect was absolutely non-existent. No matter how much people hurt me,

I remained the smiley, kind, generous woman, to the point of comforting the woman that had broken my marriage in my heavily pregnant state. This had to stop. He eventually cheated on Anita and out of spite, she spilled the beans that she was not the only one. Felix didn't come clean about all of his wrongdoing. He only confessed to the puzzle pieces that he was caught with. As the saying goes, 'he was not sorry, he was sorry he got caught'. I did not hesitate for one second and expelled him out of our common home and two days later, I filed for divorce.

Exactly two weeks before the discovery of the infidelity, I had lost my wedding ring. Felix was angry at me and he told me back then that I didn't respect our marriage by not looking hard enough for it. The same day of the discovery, I reminded him that he was quite the hypocrite to accuse me of not respecting our marriage, with this new-found knowledge of his utter disrespect. In self-defence, he replied that he respected our marriage as he always took his wedding ring off and put it in his pocket when he was having intercourse with these women, thereby respecting me. I was perplexed.

In my world, moral principles prevail over comfort and finance. Did the lack of cuddles and love in Felix' childhood contribute to him not being able to understand right from wrong and thereby explain this huge lack of respect towards me and my children? Felix should have known better. Felix could have talked to me before consciously touching another woman. Felix had many opportunities before taking that extra step to meet one of the many women he ended up cheating with. He decided with full consciousness that he was going to step beyond the moral boundary. Felix does not drink alcohol so unfortunately for him, he could not blame his actions on that. Was I really this naive to be played for years without noticing? How much more could a human being take? Was it even possible to be hurt this much? How could a man that witnessed me at my most vulnerable state dare to break my heart again? I was baffled. Did Felix ever love me or was the saviour complex going to haunt me during the rest of our marriage? How could he take me for granted all of these years? Had I accepted it because I didn't know any better? How can a father and husband who seemed to have it all, consciously decide one day to go on that downward spiral? Was he too busy focusing on the little things that were wrong, that he couldn't see the big things that were right? The thoughts and questions that I asked myself were relentless.

As the months passed, I started to self-analyse and really question whether it was truly heartbreak that I felt? Why was I attracted to Felix in the first place? Why did I attract people into my life that end up hurting me? Were the foundations which I received as a child so distorted that they didn't allow me to judge people's true intentions? Had this relationship been deceptive all along? This self-analysis takes years to complete and will most probably remain with open questions, and that is just fine. Surprisingly, Felix showed no remorse and seemed very justified in his wrongdoing. It may sound like a familiar betrayal. He got in touch with my psychologist and told her what I had discovered. She comforted him and let him know that there was no need to feel bad about it. It had to happen sooner or later due to Mary's 'background'.

My past had nothing to do with Felix' adultery. I was not impacted in any way by it and yet, it seemed like a very convenient excuse to hide behind it instead of showing remorse. In uttering those words, my psychologist at the time gave Felix the confidence and righteousness that his adultery was not too grave, and by that, dismissed any feeling of sadness, heartbreak and anger that I felt over the situation. Needless to say, that I could never trust that psychologist again either. She had ensured that would be the case. To add to this and as a sign of deep disrespect, Felix decided to hire the most expensive, media controversial lawyer in the country. The same lawyer that had defended Nicolas. Both Felix and Nicolas visited that lawyer's office on many occasions with the common aim – to break me. Felix had been there at each trial and yet this seemed to mean nothing to him now.

My decision to give Felix a second chance would have been different, had he come clean after an innocent drunken kiss at a work Christmas party with one of his female colleagues. To make matters worse, his family fully supported him and let me down. I found myself alone, heavily pregnant with three young children. Felix went back to live with his parents at nearly 40 years of age for over a year. My obstetrician was very concerned for the health of my unborn baby given the emotional shock that I had received. Since my doctor knew about my abuse history, he was angry that Felix dared hurting me this way. My doctor felt protective over me and let me know that he would refuse entry to Felix into my maternity room if that was my wish. After discovering Felix' true face, I simply could not bear for him to see me in my intimacy after giving birth as that was exactly what he had violated.

I was left to struggle as an adult on my own, but you know what, I made it through. I was used to being in survival mode and functioning on very little sleep. It was very familiar to me and I just got on with it. The day before giving birth, I was sat next to Felix in front of the judge who, with one simple sentence casually dissolved our 10-year marriage. The following day, I drove myself to the hospital with the full force of my contractions pounding in through my uterus and gave birth to my perfect fifth baby on my own.

As I am writing this, nearly two years on from the shock discovery of that infamous message, nobody from my substitute family that seemed to love me all those years, has asked me whether I needed any assistance, be it physical, emotional or financial. None of these people that seemed to care for me, and my children turned up in shame of what Felix had done and condoned his actions. In fact, I was made to feel like I had done wrong. I was the guilty party. I had no support network whatsoever and they knew that. The only safe haven that I still had left had suddenly disappeared once again because I chose moral values over everything else. Yet again, I felt the rejection from a family that apparently only loved me when I conformed, omitting my self-respect. I assume I was accepted as long as I put up with any disrespect. This felt very familiar to me. No matter how kind and innocent I was and how much pain Felix had inflicted upon me, blood came first.

If, in the future, I discover that one of my sons has cheated on his wife, let alone his heavily pregnant wife, I can assure you that I will pull him by his ear and tell him off for his wrongdoing. I will make him apologise to his wife and I will support her first before supporting him. Whether he's my child or not, principles come first. It's these principles that map out what we will accept and not accept in life, how we allow others to treat us and how we value ourselves and other people. They underpin everything.

I had no parents to protect me, nobody was there to tell me that I deserved better than Felix and that what he did was absolutely unacceptable. There was no emotional, physical, spiritual or financial support but I managed. My survival tools were sharpened within me and ready to utilise and do everything I could to minimise the instability in my children's lives. We all moved to another house with a garden, to ensure that they didn't have to change schools. I turned up four days after giving birth to a job interview in front of a panel of six renowned experts. My hair was styled, my make-up was spot on and smart clothing enveloped my slim figure. During the interview, my head was foggy, and I apologised for not being able to answer a simple scientific question. I revealed to the panel that I had pushed a 4 kg baby out of my body just four days prior. They couldn't believe it. It's amazing what the right mindset in my survival mode allowed me to accomplish.

As the months passed, Felix and his lawyer tried their best to break me financially. Much to their disappointment, I was unbreakable and always rebounded stronger than ever. Trying to keep my head above waters, I developed chronic insomnia. I was juggling work, children, including a new baby, and a household on my own full time, all the while maintaining a smile on my face. I pushed my body, mind and soul to the extreme to survive and to make ends meet. I never stopped or rested, always thinking about plan B, C and D to keep going regardless. It felt to me that my mind and body were totally disconnected. My body was struggling to keep up, but my mind was in total denial that something was wrong. That superhuman drive to survive and the deep unconditional love for my children made me carry on, on very little sleep, if at all. I put everyone first, including my children. Their emotional stability came before my health and their happiness was worth everything that I was struggling with physically. I was determined to give them the carefree childhood that I never had the chance to experience. They would grow up happy and loved - that was my mission despite their father's shortcomings. That chronic stressful state I found myself in was not by choice. I was forced into a situation that was extremely difficult and I didn't have the support system I needed so that I could sometimes delegate and rest.

Despite the struggles, the immense pride I felt every evening after a working day, when locking the front door behind me with my children safely inside my house was priceless. That daily satisfaction was worth every difficulty I had since discovering the infidelity. In case you are reading this and believe that you can't possibly take that extra step in divorcing your spouse, I'd like to reassure you that you will be fine. You will find your freedom and happiness that you compromised for the sake of the children or simply for comfort. You deserve to be happy. Your children deserve to be happy. If the post-divorce custody arrangement is fair on everyone, they will be happy, even if it means having two homes. Life is too short to be stuck in an unhappy marriage 'for the children' while trading your happiness. They need calm parents and often you will only realise in hindsight that it is for the best. Felix' infidelity was definitely the trigger and I would probably never have felt the courage to divorce, as I would be the one 'breaking up the family' but my family is far from broken. Constant arguments between parents will not make children feel stable and at peace.

For whatever reason you feel stuck in your current toxic relationship, be it infidelity or incompatibility, call it a day. Abuse is often sweetly packaged and rarely shows an aggressive side. Be it verbal, psychological, emotional or physical abuse, the offender often does it in a very loving way so that you convince yourself that he or she is not that bad after all. Let me tell you that it is very hard to recognise manipulation, sometimes referred to as gas-lighting and if you're anything like me, and have grown up to be a kind, smiley people pleaser then you easily forgive and forget, time and time again.

I am in a way glad that Felix took that immature step and did what he did. I had never tasted freedom before that. I went from one controlling relationship to the next. Even though, Felix seemed to be the type of husband that was laid back and easy going, consciously or not, he was just as controlling, coercive and wanted to know every move that I took and the details of every person I had contact with. After our divorce, I received a message from Felix accusing me of sleeping with another man. He apparently had an application on his phone that was tracking my weighing scales at home. He seemingly wanted to supervise the evolution of my weight, very caring indeed. He told me that I couldn't possibly be 76 kg as his phone had alerted him and it was necessarily a man. He was very embarrassed when my pregnant friend kindly explained to him that she had used my scales. I always felt the need to update him on my whereabouts and plans. On the other hand, I had no idea who he was spending time with or places he frequented as it turned out years later. I granted him free evenings and weekends to relax on his own away from our family life.

Felix rarely gave me attention and his contribution to the household and childcare was minimal, even though I was working full time, I felt like a single mother in my marriage. After each birth, I was up and running the household one day postpartum with my baby in a sling. There was no empathy, no proposition of taking over and the night duties were all mine. At the same time, I felt happy as I had built my own family. Felix rarely gave me compliments. Apart from Luke, I was not used to a man saying he likes my eyes, my kindness or just simply looking at me with love-filled eyes. It will take time until I am able to reply with a simple 'thank you' when a man compliments me instead of jokingly telling him to stop lying. Felix and I rarely argued which seemed too good to be true. Disputes are part of a healthy relationship. When partners don't argue at all, it may be a sign of a lack of consideration for each other. Considering the lack of love I received during my childhood and adolescence, my expectations for a husband/wife relationship were accordingly low. Another woman would most probably not have endured this kind of marriage for ten years, but I did. Perhaps Felix felt like I 'owed' him for standing by me during those four years, perhaps his saviour complex ran so deeply, and he could never get past the 'victim' image he had met me in. I was never a victim but a survivor, a very important nuance between these two terms.

Understandably, once one starts to self-analyse, the view of one's marriage becomes completely distorted. Felix never needed to seek the approval of a future father-in-law. Only his family attended the wedding while my side was empty. There comes a certain nonchalance when you don't have to 'fight' for your prey. Felix had it easy, he never had to convince my father that he was the right man for me. I'd imagine if I had parents and they found out that their son in law had hurt their pregnant daughter, they would have protected me. They would have stood by me and give Felix a hard time for playing their daughter for years. Felix, however, indirectly knew that there would be no repercussions for him if the existence of his double life came out in the open. Nobody would be there to protect me and tell him off, so he freely dared to play around.

Unfortunately, when one cheats on their partner, they also cheat on their children. I struggled to understand how one could lead a double life for years and not feel any remorse about it. How can a father come home to his wife and his children after being intimate with a stranger in a car or a hotel room only half an hour prior? It seems that what is morally wrong for most people can easily be justified for others. How can one look at himself in the mirror and at the same time live a total lie? I may be too fixated on moral values and perhaps I am not following the evolution of modern society where adultery is acceptable? Perhaps my idea of a monogamous marriage was very old fashioned? Since Felix' family didn't think that what their son did was too bad and that life goes on, I felt very confused about how one can brush this off and not stand for what is morally the right thing to do.

I didn't know what freedom was until 23 months ago. I now can buy whatever I want without having to seek out a second opinion from someone who held the final say. I can decide to drive anywhere my heart desires without justifying it to anyone. I can follow my instinct and take the decisions that I feel are right for myself and my children without questioning them. That freedom that an 18-year-old has when they finally pass their driving test is something, I never had a taste of until after my divorce.

If you think you can never trust nor love another person again, let me tell you that it's possible, even with a 'single mum of many' stamp on one's forehead. After my divorce, I indeed met a kind single father, who also understood what it was like to be out of society's mould. David has sparkling blue eyes, a beautiful smile and adorable twin daughters. He likes classy cats and despises an empty fridge. This relationship is the first one I have ever had in which I was free. The healthy foundations were in the right place this time and I was not blinded by distorted values from the past. With my divorce, I knew what I will not accept for myself ever again. I finally gave myself the respect that I deserved and would not settle for less. The world was my oyster, I felt. No matter how many times your trust has been misused, it is in your hands to trust again. You can love again, even if you believe that you will never be able to. You can rebuild a loving relationship with a new partner, there are plenty of fish in the sea. Letting go of the negative feelings is the only way to move on, nobody can do that for you but yourself.

Even though it seems that when you forgive you are doing it for the person that hurt you, you are in fact doing it for yourself. Holding on to anger, jealousy and sadness will only hurt you, not the other person. It is very hard to let go but it's doable and that is what I am working on. Life is too short, and every day is precious as I have learnt first-hand. I will not waste my thoughts and health on something I can't change. I will look for my own happiness and that of my children. I will surround myself with people that give me joy and comfort and get rid of those that my instinct tells me are of no added value in my life. After every hardship, comes the filtering. Over the years, with each struggle, I review my 'friends'. Some remain on the list, others simply go. You will only know who your friends really are when you are struggling. When everything goes well, it is not very apparent who loves you and who doesn't so much.

Today, I have no negative feelings left towards Felix. We have a kind co-parenting relationship. The children are happy and understand the new setting of having two homes. With this new family model increasingly becoming a new norm, my children do not feel out of place growing up. One of Felix' favourite TV shows was *Dragons' Den*, in which a handful of investors interrogate hopeful entrepreneurs to check their marketable potential. Felix used to tell me that it would be great if I could make use of my skills and knowledge in order to invent a product so that we both can work less and get rich that way.

Many years later, I finally took his request to heart and wrote a book from scratch. I trust that he will be proud of me for creating at last.

❦

Chapter Four

*You never know how strong you are
until being strong is the only choice you have.*
Cayla Mills

This can't be happening.

The walls are white and cold. I am sitting in the corner of the waiting area silently observing what is happening in front of me. Staff in white is rushing through the long, lonely corridor entering and exiting rooms. The people waiting with me are double my age and I can't tell if they are smiling or not under their face mask. We are all here for the same purpose. I am terrified of what is awaiting me, it is my first round, and I don't know what to expect.

A year had passed since breaking up with Felix and I found my new equilibrium in life, it was just me and my children. I felt good in my new relationship with David, we had the best of both worlds. We dated during childfree evenings and each of us had their own house and could educate our respective children the way we saw fit. There would be no disputes about daily chores. I felt that I was managing well. I could not afford a nanny at this point and tried my best to keep everything going. Christmas came around and I treated myself to a *Fitbit*, a fitness tracker, although the main purpose was definitely not to track any fitness. I realised that I would make 10,000 steps within a few hours without even trying. It's not surprising, I had a baby and three young children. In addition, at that time I also worked all day on my feet, so it was justifiable.

Shortly after starting using my *Fitbit*, I noticed that my resting heart rate was on average between 120 and 140 beats per minute, even when lying down in bed. This started to worry me as I knew that the average resting heart rate should be between 60 and 100 beats per minute, mostly around the 80 mark. I assumed this had been the case for a very long time, only now with the watch I had become aware of it as it was a visual reminder. My heart was working too hard and I became worried that I would collapse one day with a heart attack or a stroke. I consulted a cardiologist and a pneumonologist. After many investigations the tests also revealed a constant rapid heart rate with shallow breathing even during my sleep. As I had no REM sleep, the increase in heart rate couldn't even be explained by that. The experts put it down to stress and I was prescribed some supplements.

I desperately investigated every sleeping aid available. Whatever I could get my hands on, I bought it. I needed to finally let my body rest and sleep. I was ready to pay whatever it took to get some long overdue restorative sleep. I even went to the hospital desperately demanding them to artificially put me to sleep and admit me for a week so I could finally rest after being awake for a solid 18 months. I knew deep down that the forced chronic stress on my body was slowly going to kill me one day. My body was struggling to keep up on a daily basis, but my mind was in total denial and was in full survival mode. It was in nonstop 'fight or flight' mode even though there was no imminent danger anymore. The immediate threats were slowly disappearing, and life was becoming more balanced. The realisation of being totally alone was causing me internal stress, when from the outside, I wasn't connected to it. Even though my substitute family and Felix were not the kind of family that was fully supportive, that placebo effect in my mind of having a back-up to catch me when I fall was there and it did the trick. This pretend back-up was now fully absent. Do not take your parents for granted however dysfunctional your family may be. They will catch you one way or another and that peace of mind gives you inner calmness that you don't know you have until it's gone.

Months went by, life was hectic but beautiful. I finally had the means to hire a nanny and found an amazing one in Anna Lee. I was starting to delegate more and more and spent the few hours I had after work enjoying quality time with my children. I started to embrace that new routine wholeheartedly and then the lock-down came around. I welcomed the break in the daily routine and spent the most wonderful few months with my children. We profited from the garden and baked, we enjoyed life slowing down from the rushed school mornings and constant hustle and bustle until bedtime. Like most parents, I also extended their screen time allowance while trying to set up my home office. I didn't feel bad about it. The pressure was omnipresent with home-schooling and remote work while single parenting four young children with no support. By the end of it, I knew all of the episodes of *Peppa Pig* by heart without ever seeing them. After unintentionally listening to them on repeat from a distance, I could repeat scenes to my children, which they were very impressed about.

One morning during that lock-down, I suddenly felt a tremendous surge of pain in my lower back which doubled me up and because of its intensity, I fell to the floor, curled up and frightened of what was happening to me. I attempted to stand up several times and kept struggling – how would I even be able to walk? My baby was crawling, and I could not lift him to walk down the stairs. Following this episode, I received medical help, numerous steroid injections and strong medication. I brushed off that incident as a flare up of my ongoing chronic lower back pain. A few weeks after that, I experienced abnormal vaginal bleeding. It concerned me a little, but I put it down to the strong painkillers, which can have blood thinning effects. I fully justified the cause of the symptom to myself and to the doctor at the time. I never seemed to put on weight proportionally to what I ate. Again, this seemed justifiable with the number of unintentional steps I was seeing on that watch – running around after several young children, keeping a home in order and working a full-time demanding job was no mean feat.

The bleeding continued and deep down my instinct told me that there was something wrong. It wasn't like any bleeding I had experienced before, the appearance of seeing the red matter regularly was panic inducing and so I decided to investigate it further. My pap smear result came back normal. Nothing to worry about there, which was a relief. After all, the likelihood of having cancer with a clear pap smear was pretty small, so I thought. After further examination, I was still bleeding, the gynaecologist discovered a large tumour high up inside my cervix that was not present at the annual check-up I had had three months prior. How could I have a large tumour when it was not there three months ago? How can a tumour have grown this fast when I gave birth 16 months ago? I had always been to my annual check-up after all. As far as my knowledge went, this check-up would have spotted an abnormality long before cancer cells could have camped in my cervix. There was no way, this tumour could be malignant. The doctor had no answer. She sent off the biopsy and reassured me that it could simply be a cervical polyp, which was very common and that it could easily be removed in an outpatient setting.

The bleeding threw up dozens of questions for me, which raced through my mind, all at once. Was the back pain perhaps related? Was my rapid heart rate indicating something more sinister than chronic stress? I started to get worried and researched more and more, convincing myself that it couldn't possibly come back as cancer as I had given birth to five children within seven years and everything that I read, stated that cervical cancer takes years to develop. The fact that my pap smear was clear was enough to convince me that the mass was benign.

I reassured myself after reading this information that it couldn't possibly be cancer. I believed in what I was telling myself and went on with my work and life as usual. The week of waiting for my result had passed and the gynaecologist called me into the clinic to talk. Strangely, that same day coincided with my daughter's third death anniversary. As I sat in the waiting area with David, an uneasy feeling was brewing up inside of me as the doctor made me wait longer than I should have for that biopsy result and specifically asked me to come in. Surely if it was a simple polyp, she would not need to speak to me face to face? My heart pounded while I was waiting to be called in. I was unconsciously used to my chronic racing heart but this time I could consciously feel it.

The doctor called us in, and just looking at her facial expression I knew that it was not good news. With tears welling up in her eyes, she announced to me that I had a rare, invasive and aggressive form of cervical cancer. Without any optimism for the prognosis or survival rate, I took this information in, without really taking it in as I was shell shocked. I looked at David, trying to gather some calmness from his facial expression, but he was just as frozen by that brutal announcement as I was. It was absolutely surreal, and I was in no way prepared to hear those words. I think nobody will ever be prepared to hear these words. I could not get myself to cry, the shock fully paralysed me for a moment. I took my results from the doctor's hand and left the room in a blur. I broke down once I got outside in front of the hospital.

How could I possibly have cancer? I was 37 years old, eating a healthy diet, never smoked and rarely drank alcohol. How could this be missed by the doctors when I have given birth through that same cervix five times in a short space of time, the last time being 16 months ago? Did she really just say I had cancer? This must be a mistake. My pap smear was normal after all. Was that annual test not supposed to pick up pre-cancerous cells long before an actual malignant tumour could develop? I was confused. I looked at David while crying uncontrollably, repeating the same sentence as if in trance. He tried to reassure me, but I knew deep down that he didn't know any more than I did about this diagnosis. I urgently needed to speak to someone else who might be able to shed more light on this news. I rushed off to see my usual gynaecologist and spilled out the devastating news I'd just been given. He tried to calm me down. He told me that my tumour was inoperable and that if the cancer had not spread, that I would need to undergo chemo- and radiotherapy to make the tumour shrink. At this point, I did not know whether the cancer had metastasised or not. The fact that the first doctor said invasive and aggressive was enough for me to project myself into a possible scenario of palliative care.

My world broke down. I called Hild and repeated down the phone about a hundred times: 'Hild, I have cancer'.

I was unconsciously uttering these words with tears flowing down my face. I felt as if I was totally detached from my body and this was happening to someone else. This could not be my new reality. I had suffered enough; I could not take any more. Life was finally stable, and I met a man that loved and respected me. Hild was feeling as helpless and tried to reassure me even if at this point, I just couldn't think rationally. The news was given to me in such a brutal way that I remained in that disbelief for some time. Even if life was unpredictable, I wanted nothing more than some sort of guarantee that I will live long enough to see my babies grow. I did not want any more than that.

All I could do was cry during that first week, it was unbearable. The waiting, the uncertainty, the immense fear of not being fortunate enough to be there for my children, it felt too much for me to take, but I convinced myself that I had to take it. There was no alternative, I was not prepared to give up believing that I had the same right to live like everyone else. Life didn't give me the honour to mother these amazing children only to take it all away from me this soon. I refused to accept that the diagnosis was going to define me. It was up to me to take action and be in control of the diagnosis, not the other way around. I knew this was key to my wellbeing.

I saw my children that evening after the brutal announcement of my diagnosis and I welcomed them with a big smile as if nothing was going on. I believe children have very smart emotional radars and they sense when something is not right. I had no idea of how I was supposed to approach this. Do I mention the word 'cancer'? Do I downplay the seriousness of the disease to not make them feel worried? They would inevitably notice that it wasn't just the usual back pain that they were used to seeing me with. They would eventually understand that people can die from cancer. I wanted to protect them by trivialising the fear I had towards death. I smiled at them and reassured them that the doctor would take good care of mummy and remove the pain in her tummy. I showed them how the second degree burn on my hand that I had gotten 2 weeks prior had healed beautifully. I explained to them that my body was working as it should to fight any pain.

David stood by me during those weeks of uncertainty, accompanying me to my appointments and scans. He was an absolute rock. He suffered with me when the news was daunting and sighed in relief with me when we received hopeful news amongst the bad ones. I feel grateful to have this man by my side and he absolutely contributes to my positive mindset. When one is faced with a diagnosis like this, one tends to jump straight to the worst-case scenario, especially when you hear it from a professional. David never let go of my hand and consistently reminded me of the positive aspects of my individual case. He kept me away from the internet with all of the daunting statistics, prognostic factors and survival rates. He was the buffer that kept me above water during these difficult weeks. He definitely didn't sign up for this much turbulence just one year after meeting me, but it seemed like life had more surprises in store for me than I thought.

After absorbing the initial shock, I went into my familiar proactive survival mode. I could not wait around for the MRI appointment that was scheduled six full weeks after the diagnosis. I had no time to lose, I was determined to get things moving and find a solution to my issue as soon as possible, no matter the distance, no matter the cost. I made sure that my children felt safe and secure with Anna and their father. I took my remaining courage and energy and drove hundreds of miles to Germany on my own to find an experienced gynaeco-oncologist, seeking a second opinion. With a different treatment approach to the previous doctors, I felt at ease with the treatment strategy and I felt that I was in good hands. Everyone is different and there is no one 'fit for all' treatment. The approach needs to be individualised and tailored. Many factors should be considered before deciding.

As Luxembourg was becoming a Covid risk zone, I decided to self-isolate in Germany for the few weeks before my surgery as catching the virus would have delayed my treatment, potentially causing the cancer to spread further, which at that point had not yet. I stayed in a hotel on my own with minimal contact to the outside world. I was constantly bouncing from a state of relief to one of absolute fear at the thought of the cancer spreading further since it had been labelled as 'aggressive' and 'invasive' by the first doctor. One evening, after dining at the restaurant in the hotel, I stood up and felt a gush of blood flowing down my legs. In full panic, I tried to remain discrete and awkwardly held my dress while slowly walking to the bathroom. The bleeding was uncontrollable, and the toilet cubicle resembled a murder scene. I had never experienced this much bleeding before, despite being familiar with postpartum bleeding. This time it was different, the tumour was massively bleeding, and it just did not stop. I frantically tried to reach the reception, evidently embarrassed in need of an ambulance. That night, lying in a hospital bed alone in a foreign country away from my children after a huge blood loss was absolutely terrifying. I imagined what if I never got the chance to say goodbye to my loved ones. I was determined to never have that scenario ever happen to me, even though we can't always control what happens to us, but we can choose how we manage it.

Few weeks following the initial diagnosis, I had a very long complicated surgery abroad that unfortunately revealed that the cancer had already spread to the lymph nodes. Waking up in the recovery room, losing all dignity and being told that the cancer was not only local but was now given the highest grade of aggressive spread, I was absolutely terrified. The cancer was now upgraded from Stage 1 to a Stage 3 within a matter of weeks. With the highest terminal stage being 4, I was not able to remain calm. I was already in a morbid mood and no words could attenuate my fears.

The cancer was very aggressive, and I was supposed to let my body recover after the surgery before attacking it further. At that point, I decided to write the book you are currently holding in your hands. What else did I have to lose than my own life? I was finally ready to publicly expose my deepest vulnerability. David came into the recovery room and was the first person I saw in my fearful, broken state. Seeing him calmed me down when he reassured me that everything would be fine. His calm nature was what I needed to get through the heavy weeks of chemo and radiotherapy that were awaiting me once I recovered from surgery. The weeks of recovery away from my children were the hardest. I was overwhelmed with fear and did not know how to handle this.

I tried to make sense of it all in order to feel in control again. At my best, I regarded this cancer diagnosis as another label I had received. The tumour had probably taken years to develop and it wasn't because it now had a name that I needed to feel 'sick' and should be treated as such. I was the same person that I was the month prior to the diagnosis. I slowly accepted the diagnosis and started talking to other cancer survivors. They gave me real life insights into cancer treatment and possible short and long-term side effects. Up until then, what I knew about cancer treatment was from my studies. I needed real people that had gone through it and came out stronger than ever.

When you get a terrifying diagnosis like this, your whole world as you know it, breaks down, as you are forced to face your own mortality. You feel like you have lost control of your own life and nothing matters anymore, the only wish you have is to live. Cancer was the last thing I expected to have but I had it and it didn't surprise me. Being in that chronic stressful 'fight or flight' mode that I found myself in since discovering the adultery, increased stress hormones such as cortisol and adrenaline, decreased the immune response and with the added extreme insomnia, the cells never got the opportunity to rest and regenerate. It only takes one dysfunctional cell that is not efficiently detoxified by a working immune system to create a cycle of indefinite cell multiplication, thereby forming a malignant tumour.

This diagnosis was a definite wake up call for me to finally look after myself and slow down. If I didn't fix my body now, then my children would grow up without a mother and I was determined to make sure that this would never happen. The adjuvant chemotherapy and radiation that followed the surgery were very difficult on me physically and emotionally. After surgically implanting a port below my collar bone, it became all very real. This foreign ball under my skin was very awkward. It was a visual reminder of the treatment awaiting me. I knew the practicality of it for the chemotherapy but the fact that I had to live with it for a few years afterwards 'just in case' was hard to swallow. When I now see a person with that scar below the collar bone with or without the port, it feels like we are part of a secret club. A club that we'd wholeheartedly unsubscribe from.

The hospital staff was friendly, and I started to develop affinities with the elderly people who were also having daily radiation and weekly chemotherapy with me. The mere fact that the medical staff put on protective gear when administering my chemotherapy infusion was enough for me to identify this liquid running into my vein as poison despite rationally knowing that it was supporting my healing. Likewise, the radiology assistants leaving the room each time I was given the thirty sessions of radiotherapy made me realise that it was way too risky for them to be in the same room as me while I was given the full radiation dose into my body.

The first week of treatment seemed to be a walk in the park. I had imagined cancer treatment to be more brutal but I felt physically fine or so I thought. I spoke too soon I figured as by that first weekend, I slowly became a messy ball of a human, unable to stand up, let alone go to the toilet by myself. The lingering nausea started, and the intense exhaustion was stronger than me. I was alone and miserable, unable to care for myself. For someone who is used to be in control of her life, this new normal was a punch in the face. I was very independent and now I was nothing or so it felt. The abrupt premature menopause didn't help me feel better about the situation. The unbearable hot flushes started, and I could not feel the cold or hot like my surrounding could. It was as if one of my children was constantly playing with my internal thermostat day and night. When people think of menopause, they assume it's all about hot flashes but there is more to it and my body was too young to live the next years without oestrogen flowing. It was crucial in the long run for my heart, bones, brain, emotional well-being and sexual health to still have oestrogen running in my veins. I didn't get the opportunity to navigate in peri-menopause after all, that radical drop in hormones was way too brutal.

This time I did not shy away from asking for help. Since I was living on my own and there was no immediate help in case, I needed it, I asked to be given a portable alarm in case of an emergency. This service is reserved for the elderly but can also be offered to younger patients living alone. I also subscribed to meals on wheels and cooked food was brought to me on a daily basis. I quickly unsubscribed to this as I had lost all appetite for cooked food. I needed to put on weight for both physical and psychological reasons. I needed to stop seeing a skinny girl in the mirror as my mind associates that image with sickness. I desperately wanted to see 5-10 kg more on me to feel healthy.

I strangely craved cold food and my perfect meal for weeks simply consisted of sticks of carrots, cucumber, bell peppers and cherry tomatoes dipped in full fat cream seasoned with salt and pepper. Pickles were also part of the menu. It somehow felt like the side effects of the treatment could be compared to a pregnancy with the extreme tiredness, the strange cravings, the lingering nausea and vomiting only without the precious gift at the end, although I'll always consider a clear negative follow up scan, a very precious gift too. I will gladly cry of joy holding a negative CT, PET or MRI scan report in my arms like new parents do holding their freshly born baby. It is a rebirth after all for the cancer patient after a long heavy treatment. It is a second chance. For some, a third or fourth chance and it can somehow be compared to 'coming from the dead' especially after a stage 3 or 4 cancer diagnosis.

Since the chemotherapy ward was filled with people that were much older than me, I felt very out of place and I felt the injustice on a daily basis. I guess seeing younger patients being in the same boat would have made me feel like I am not alone in this. I used to talk to everyone in the waiting room although the mask was making it even more difficult to break the ice but we quickly as a society adapted to this new normal. I enjoyed listening to my co-warriors telling me stories from their childhood. My weekly hospital room neighbour Geraldine was very lovely. She has four boys, and she is exactly forty years older than me. Her treatment plan was the same as mine following surgery and her stubborn will to survive despite having to drive back and forth over an hour every day during six weeks of heavy treatment was a very good lesson to me. No matter the age, you've never lived enough to call it a day. That determination to get through any adversity no matter the age is very admirable.

On many occasions, David came to my weekly chemotherapy sessions and simply sat beside me while the infusion made its way into my body. He was a very welcome distraction to my current reality, and we used to fill those moments with jokes and laughter. Making guesses about the lyrics of the infusion pump was one of our weekly games. The countless side effects stemming from the cancer treatment were slowly wearing me down. Half-way through the treatment, I just couldn't take that state anymore, it felt like it was never ending, and I was emotionally exhausted from being physically broken and not being able to feel human.

I felt very disconnected from real life. It was as if I was living in a parallel state while life continued outside with everyday worries. I could not relate to people's worries anymore; my empathy hit a wall. Despite the world outside changing with the new virus causing uncertainties and shaking the world at its foundations, I was very jealous of these people that worried about simple things while I was sat there unable to move, eat or sleep, fearful of what was still to come. Sadly, it seemed that many people around me confused the side effects of the treatment with symptoms of cancer and treated me accordingly with pity. Since cancer is mostly invisible and doesn't produce symptoms unless it's advanced, the patient tends to only suffer when he or she is under treatment. The weight and hair loss, the nausea and vomiting, the intense fatigue, the pale face unfortunately give the patient a 'sick' look while, without treatment, the patient may feel and look fit. These symptoms come across as disease progression and people often forget that it is the treatment that causes the suffering and not the disease itself. As with many injuries, one must remember that it gets worse before it gets better. David never left my side and kept my spirits high, he counted down the sessions with me and was the best cheerleader that I could possibly have wished for.

Strangely enough, the last week of treatment was the hardest on me emotionally when logically I should have been relieved. It was as if I was dreading the hole I was going to fall into after months of being taken care of. I was somehow worried about being left alone with my fears. I knew that I needed to build a support network to surround me post treatment. I admitted myself into a wonderful post-oncological rehabilitation centre, which helped me regain my forces after the end of the treatment. The programme is tailor made to each patient's needs and is a good transition before going back to a routine at home and work. The added value offered by all the professionals on site is priceless and I can highly recommend it. The network of physiotherapists, doctors, nurses, dieticians, psychologists and social workers aims at providing the patient with a comprehensive set of tools to take home. The centre I attended was situated in the middle of nature, which allowed me to walk in the forest and feel grounded again.

I had great apprehension of my children seeing me as 'sick' while being in treatment. I needed to learn that I don't always have to put my 'superhuman' mask on. I am allowed to have pain and show it. I don't want them to grow up thinking that they need to be perfect at all times. I keep reminding my children that they are allowed to make mistakes because mummy makes mistakes too. One Sunday morning, the children asked me whether they can also draw the radiation marks on their tummy along with the scar and the port. I drew the same marks I had on their little body and despite it being a casual game, it was deeper than that. That day, they felt included in my pain without actually having pain. It was symbolically very healing for me and for them too I imagine. As the new coronavirus was causing trouble outside and a simple infection could be life-threatening for a person in cancer treatment, I had that additional fear to deal with as my immune system became more and more compromised with each passing week.

The children are now growing in a world that is filled with people in masks and gloves with no facial expressions that is essential for learning and social interactions at an early age. Despite my biggest fears, I simply could not stay in a mask 24/7 around my children, they needed to be comforted by my smile, showing that everything was fine even when it wasn't at all times. We sometimes expect way too much from our children. We expect them to have adult rational thinking and behaviour when it took us 30 years to know what we know now. We tend not to give them the time needed to fall and learn. They grow up thinking that they disappoint us when they don't conform. I tell my children that they are allowed to be sad, angry, jealous or frustrated. They are allowed to cry when they hurt. I encourage open communication and free expression of emotions.

Boys can play with dolls if they wish to. They can dress up as Elsa from *Frozen* if they choose to. How do we expect boys to develop paternal affection if they grow up with the idea that parental affection is only reserved for girls? Society subconsciously contributes to the fact that we find ourselves in a world where mothers are seen to be the only competent carers for children, while fathers are expected to only play rough and 'babysit'. They are praised for doing simple chores related to childcare as if they were doing the mother a favour. Perhaps we should rethink how these gender specific toys at an early age are affecting the pool of fathers we end up with in the future. Perhaps it is time, we let children choose what they want to play with. Perhaps it is time that we don't giggle at boys playing with pretend babies and encourage girls to play with toys that promote logical thinking. We want equality between parents, let's start by giving children equal chances from an early age. Let's not assume that every girl likes pink and glitter while every boy loves *Lego* and cars.

We should look our children in the eyes and treat them the way we want to be treated. We should not undermine their intelligence just because they are small in size. They understand more than we give them credit for. They are worth every physical and emotional pain I am currently feeling and going through. By the end of it, I will not have lived with my children for many months, but the reunion back home will be ever so sweet because of that. The mere vision of this reunion is hugely motivating for me to hang on in there. Even though I miss them more than words can ever describe, I remind myself why this break is happening. I must look after myself first before I can look after my children, in order to be the fittest version of myself. I will make sure I never run on an empty tank again. I am grateful for the new technologies that allow me to stay in contact with my children. Their endless love declarations warm my heart and are a constant reminder of the four most beautiful reasons why this battle is necessary. I observe my children and can't believe that they are mine. I am in awe. I look at them talking, often they say absolute nonsense and I realise that they are the same tiny babies that I used to comfort for hours at night. I am a lucky mummy.

One of my absolute favourite children's book is *Mon amour* by Astrid Desbordes. The underlying message in the book is pure unconditional love. The book is short and sweet. I always tell my children that my favourite page of the book is the one which says that I love them when I see them, when they are with me and I love them when I don't see them, when they are with their father for example. Especially for children of divorced parents, this message is very important as they tend to feel unstable with this back and forth between the co-parents.

I may have missed milestones of my baby's development, but my lovely nanny keeps me updated with photos and videos that keep me smiling. I feel very grateful to have found her just before the lockdown. Sometimes, people come into your life and the timing is perfect without really knowing what lies ahead. She is a blessing. Thanks to her, my children can play in my house every day, sleep in their own beds, have a little bit of normality and not feel like they have moved to stay with their father for many months. They get to feel at home every day and that means a lot to me. I consciously try to continually reassure them that everything will be fine, and life will go back to normal albeit at a slower rhythm for me.

After each life struggle, people would tell me how 'unlucky' I was. My smiley reply would always be that no, I am very lucky. I am surrounded by beautiful children, who are growing up in a happy home. I couldn't ask for more than that. The perspective of people on your life can put you down and be very opposed to how you feel about your own life. Gratitude comes with struggles. The more you have to overcome, the more you'll appreciate how beautiful life really is and how fortunate you really are. It is very easy to take people and things for granted. The saying that you'll only appreciate the value of something once it's gone, is indeed very true.

Even though I definitely didn't need another wake-up call to appreciate the beautiful world that we live in, I definitely needed that imposed break that I am going through right now. Even if I wanted, I couldn't physically be tempted to do more than my body allows me. I am grateful for each moment that I get to spend with my precious children. I will take care of ME now. It's now or never. I have always been in a hyper vigilance mode that never allowed my body and mind to truly relax. I needed to be in that chronic alert state since I was a child because I was harmed every day and it was my self-protection. That readiness to fight danger has remained into adulthood and I am very aware of this requiring immediate change in order to get my body to finally rest.

What other people take for granted with the deep breathing, I need to learn again. I need to unlearn this shallow breathing that has my heart working too hard. There is no danger anymore and I need to convince my mind that I am safe, my children are safe and that is all that matters. I consciously walk slowly with no rush as I always used to race about everywhere. I consciously tell myself that my to-do list can wait and there will be reminders for invoices if I don't pay immediately. I must not always have all my to-do tasks ticked off. These to-do lists used to give me a sense of control and inner peace when they were checked. My house always had to be in order, no matter how tired I was. I couldn't possibly go to bed when the house was untidy. It resembled more like an obsessive-compulsive disorder, even though for me, it was simply a way of feeling that if my home was orderly, so was my inner peace. We all try to find foundations and since I didn't have anything healthy and solid to rely on, I created my own standards for feeling secure, no matter how absurd they may seem on the outside.

Since having children, I have been plagued with mummy guilt. I constantly felt that I was letting my children down because I always went back to work sooner than other mothers at school. Society has a subtle way of making working mothers feel like they are not being the best mothers to their children because the children go to childcare. Likewise, stay at home mothers are made to feel worthless because apparently, they don't contribute to the household income, and in the wider sense to the national economy. It doesn't matter whether you stay at home to raise your children or go to work every day, neither will ever feel right. Especially after divorcing, I found myself in a situation of being the sole provider of the household income. I have learnt to accept that despite it not being ideal, it was the only solution to keep my head above water with four young children on my own. I think the mummy guilt will never fully disappear. Even now, going through a heavy journey, I am feeling guilty for not being with my children. I must repeat to myself that I am doing this for the long-term benefit. I must fix myself now so that I can be the best mother I can for years to come. The time away from them during my cancer treatment is a short-term pain for a long-term gain.

I need to relearn human reflexes that I had seemingly lost. I could not yawn, no matter how exhausted I was. I could not feel any fatigue in my constantly wired state, and I envied people who were tired, yawning and who fell asleep within a few minutes. I wanted this so badly. I attended a trauma sensitive yoga course and started yawning a lot during the class. I apologised to the instructor because I was embarrassed about it. She told me with a smile that this is exactly what she wanted to see, as the yawning signals that the body is relaxing. I owe it to my body to take care of it after the battering it had taken. It has carried five beautiful children and has gotten me through decades of pain. I will respect it and love it as I should have all along. I will give it the rest it needs to recharge and slow down my heart. I will not find excuses to put off the breathing exercises and rehabilitation after the surgery, chemotherapy and radiation. It is now time to reconnect body, mind and soul and to feel the extreme tiredness that my mind was in total denial of. I am proud of my body that it has carried me all of these years despite the countless hardships. At the initial diagnosis, the feeling that my body had betrayed me was immense. Today, I don't feel this way. I thank my body for enduring all this pain from the surgery and cancer treatment and rebounding to allow me to live on.

I have never developed a healthy relationship with food and I rarely took the time to cook for myself. My self-love was non-existent. Everyone else came before my own needs. I was not important enough, and I used to eat anything on the go, albeit still making healthy choices. This will definitely change going forward and I will take the time to give my body the best nutrients that it deserves to thrive. Like many people finding themselves confronted with a cancer diagnosis, I also got myself a juicer and started researching how I could prevent a recurrence of the disease in the future. I had the urge to be proactive about it. I wanted to avoid hearing another brutal sentence anytime soon. I promised myself that I will treat my body with the respect it deserves after carrying me all these years. My body did not fail me as I thought when I first heard the word 'cancer'. I am nearly inclined to thank this cancer for coming into my life, despite having wished for a gentler form of a wake-up call. A local, common, slow growing cancer could have been enough for me to wake up, I seriously did not need to add more complexity to the situation. Apparently even in cancer, I was given the more difficult version, it had to be a rare and aggressive one. Regardless, I was ready to overcome this period of my life at any cost.

The overwhelming, often contradictory, information about cancer prevention is now filling my bookshelves. There is obviously a big market opportunity when one plays on the fear of existence of cancer patients. We are an easy prey. If someone had asked me many months before whether I believed in certain re-purposed drugs and natural supplements as having anti-cancer activity, I would not have been too convinced unless I saw evidence-based research. Today, I am a big fan of alternative treatments backed up by scientific research when used as an adjunctive treatment to conventional cancer drug therapy. The internet is a big pile of unfiltered information and if someone finds themselves catapulted from one day to the other in this unknown parallel world of cancer, it can be incredibly overwhelming and fearful. Please stay away from the net.

Getting a diagnosis like this changes you forever. I will most likely always have the inner fear at the back of my mind that the cancer will eventually return. That grey cloud over my head following me will hopefully slowly disintegrate with time. With each follow-up scan showing no evidence of disease, NED as we say in the cancer community, my inner peace will slowly grow. I will not be officially 'healed' unless my body shows that it has been cancer free for five years at least. I can imagine that I will be even more vigilant about new symptoms than I was before. I will most likely have more frequent check-ups just to put my mind at ease. I will help my body be in the best physical condition to fight recurrence. I am very determined to survive this, and I have no doubt that I will. I will ask for help. I will guiltlessly delegate more and rest. I will treat myself to the quiet carefree life that I deserve.

It goes without saying that once you're faced with your own mortality, your whole perspective in life changes. I have always been a people pleaser. I had trouble uttering NO with each request at work or socially, never honouring a no if that was what my soul dearly wanted. I would go to events that I didn't want to go to. I took great care of other people's feelings, doing anything to prevent hurting them, and more importantly, I wanted to be liked. That was the absolute aim. I usually tried my hardest as energy consuming as it was and it's easy to see where this feeling originates from. When you don't have parents, or anyone for that matter, to back you up, you feel like you need to please everyone and have trouble filtering the ones that truly love you, from the ones that are taking advantage of your kindness. This need is wired deeply into my core having learnt it at a very young age. I am finally at a point in my life where I am able to see what people's intentions truly are. Always follow your gut feeling, it is usually right. If you feel that a person doesn't truly want the best for you, then it is most probably the case. The more that you trust your inner guide, and the more you practice it, the more natural this process becomes, as it should.

I now consciously question myself whether I am putting myself first. I still have moments that I am angry at myself for falling into the people pleaser mode again but at least I am now increasingly conscious of which behaviour I need to change. It will take time to get rid of this unhealthy reflex of always putting everyone else before my needs. Baby steps.

Over the years, I have learnt that people expect to see a certain image with a person going through a specific struggle. Unfortunately, when one doesn't conform to the expected image, the empathy received is often absent. I have heard it over and over again that I seem less credible because I don't look like I am suffering to an outsider. Up until today, I make the extra effort each and every day to not fall into the victim 'look'. No matter how much I was suffering inside, be it physical or emotional pain, I pulled myself up, put on a nice dress, my hair would be groomed, make up applied and I smiled at the world. It may seem very superficial but the healing from any adversity starts in the mind. If I look at myself in the mirror and I like what I see, my body will believe it too. I learnt to smile at myself in the mirror, it is very powerful. I remind myself with stickers on my mirror that I am worth it, and I can do anything if the inner will is there.

On the other hand, if I let the adversity in life take over, I would most probably have fallen into a deep depression by now. I certainly would have enough reasons to do so. It's very mundane, but you too, even if you don't feel like it, you don't have to fall into the expected image of the victim. Make that little effort every day to look after yourself and smile. As a lovely friend of mine, Caroline Emile told me, I may not be able to control what happens to me, but it's fully in my hands to choose what happens next. She also reminded me that I should not deprive myself from fun and happiness no matter what is going on in life. We tend to feel that we should not be enjoying ourselves or be happy, simply because we are going through a rough journey. On the contrary, when we are happy, the immune system is boosted. Caroline, before starting her chemotherapy, threw a pre-chemo party and went into the heavy battle with red lipstick, red nail polish and most importantly a smile. She was making sure that she was constantly giving her immune system the boost it needed to overcome the therapy.

Caroline inspired me and this was exactly the mindset that I have embarked on this heavy journey with. As I have shown before, I refuse to fall into the 'victim' image. I am fully motivated to get through this. I surround myself with strong men and women that have survived a similar journey. They empower me to beat this cancer wholeheartedly. If unfortunately, you have found yourself in my shoes, I strongly advise you to look for like-minded people that have gone through or are currently enduring the same battle. It is worth gold and makes the world of difference. I have never been a big social media fan, but I can definitely see the benefit of it in times like these. I have connected with people from all over the world.

The solidarity from strangers gives me faith in humanity. Strangers helping other strangers who find themselves in the same boat provides an amazing strength. Regardless of the personal struggle, there are others out there who are currently suffering like you and whom you can identify with. They have the same, or similar fears and worries, that keep them up at night and physical pains in common. There are also the ones who are years ahead of you. It is very comforting and reassuring to talk to people that give you the hope that you need to cling onto. Surrounding yourself with people, who also faced the same pain but are now in remission, living a full and vibrant life is crucial. It is sometimes easier said than done, but each one of us can find that little piece of remaining strength within that can make all the difference.

Evidently, it is sometimes easier to fall into a 'victim' role and act like society expects you to while receiving the sympathy that comes with it. It is of course inevitable in the beginning. I have also had a week of 'victimhood' after each announcement of bad news because the emotional pain and the overwhelming fear, simply took over any pragmatic thinking I usually have and practise. We are not super humans nor robots. We are vulnerable and fragile. After that week of fully embracing the desperation, my action mode needed to be switched on and this switch actively contributed to helping me move forward. I don't see any added value in remaining in a 'victim' state for a long time. People may empathise with you and empathy is human. It is at the core of the majority of society and is what is required immediately after receiving bad news. Having people around you that care and have an understanding softens the blow and helps in those shocking days that follow. However, after a while, this empathy will only cause a person that is trying very hard to actively contribute to their healing to be set back. It has no added value anymore as it will only serve to remind the person that his or her situation is sad and unfair.

I totally understand how family and friends can feel helpless when faced with such a situation. It is not easy to say the right things at the right time. There are no words to describe the pain that the cancer patient is feeling. Your friend or relative may start to isolate themselves and not reply to your messages. It is a very human reaction to not want to have contact with anyone after such a blow. A person might be trying to make sense of the situation and any 'wrong' statement from someone may trigger a very emotional reaction. It is very confusing for well-meaning people to then know what the right approach to take so as not to hurt their friend or relative. Rest assured that there is no right way of approaching this delicate situation. It may sound absurd, but a simple headache may equal 'brain metastases' for a cancer patient. In my head, a new symptom is directly related to disease recurrence or progression. Instead of minimising the genuine fear of your friend or relative, please treat it with the uttermost understanding. Once one's own existence has been threatened, the perception of common symptoms will never be as before the diagnosis. Sometimes we are only limited to what we can offer as advice to someone receiving such a heavy diagnosis. Sometimes saying, 'you will get through this' often doesn't resonate with someone in the middle of cancer. My immediate thought when someone says this is, 'how do you know it will be okay?' I rationally wonder how the well-meaning person can guarantee that everything will turn out just fine? If someone who's been through the same journey tells me 'you'll be fine', it feels more credible. Sometimes saying nothing and just being there is better than saying the wrong thing at the wrong time.

At the time of writing this, I have known my diagnosis for 14 weeks and it is very surprising to me how many well-meaning people have told me about someone they know that has died of cancer. This is an absolute no-go. You do not tell someone who is potentially facing their own mortality that you had a work colleague, friend, aunt, neighbour or parent that has succumbed to cancer. How do you think that affects the person hearing this? Where does it leave them to go from here, with any hope or inspiration wiped out with one thoughtless sentence? I do not represent the prostate cancer of your grandfather nor the pancreatic cancer of your uncle. Each person has their own cancer, and this pathology is so diverse that there is no point comparing my cancer to anyone else's. That is one of the reasons why I started isolating myself more and more because statements like those just remind me of my own vulnerability. Instead, if you really want to calm your friend or relative, tell them about someone you know that has survived cancer and is doing great 5 or 10 years later.

Another comment that kept irritating me was the casual question 'what do the doctors say/think?' I did not understand at first why this question was making me uncomfortable. One day, during the 12-hour infusion into my port, I extensively thought about the reason why this question bothered me so much. I came to the conclusion that this question is never asked when the diagnosis is asthma or diabetes for example, as these are not associated with mortality. The perception of society when it comes to cancer is different and the strong link to death is very clear. If someone asks me 'what do the doctors think?', I unfortunately translate this in my head as being asked whether I am going to be cured or not, which is another way of asking whether I will live or die. This question has no added value to the patient and all it does is bring someone down that may already be very down and is only trying to push themselves forward.

Apparently 1 in 2 people will be diagnosed with cancer sooner or later. That is vast. I may know something now that I didn't know for 10 years. I probably had the beginnings of cancer during my pregnancies too. We all have cancer cells floating around in our body, but they are efficiently continuously disposed of by a functioning immune system. You currently may not know it, but you also may have cancer and you just don't know about it yet. It is not because it suddenly is written on a report that you become 'sick'. I see myself as someone with a condition that is treatable, and I am in no way defining myself as 'sick'. Just like any other chronic disease, I will have regular follow ups and I will keep my condition under control. We all forget how vulnerable we are and that we are facing daily risks every day, even life-threatening ones. There are no guarantees in life. We would live in fear if we focused on what could go wrong and make it more likely for it to manifest itself into reality.

As another beautiful friend of mine, Iman, reminded me that unless I am on my knees, I still had a choice. I received debilitating news many weeks ago. What I do with the news was now up to me. I must ask myself, am I sick now? Am I on my knees now? Am I dying now? The answer is NO to all of those questions and that is when the determination of fighting back starts. Unless I am really on my knees, not able to stand up because I am really sick, that's when I will call myself sick, and even then, I will most likely be that same determined fighter. Today, I am fully capable of taking full action to contribute towards my fate.

Chapter Five

*Attitude is a little thing that
makes a big difference.*
Winston Churchill

The second wave.

The walls are white and cold. I am sitting in a waiting room with this familiar overwhelming fear. Around me, people are talking about the second wave. I can relate on a different level. My second wave is also beginning. It's a Deja-vu that I feel more in control of, although the extent of the collateral damage is still undetermined. The medical staff invites me into the scanning facility and my heart is pounding.

A few weeks had passed after the last treatment and I was slowly regaining my appetite and energy. My children were back in my arms and I felt happy and complete. I was finally done sorting the administrative side of the disease. The medical bills piling up were not all covered by my health insurance. I found dealing with the bureaucracy while being physically broken very overwhelming. I should have dedicated one person to this task. The fear at the back of my mind still being very fresh, I continued exchanging with my psychotherapist on a regular basis. I joined a post oncological sports group through which I got to know people that had gone through cancer treatment. I decided to integrate exercise into my life and quickly realised that I didn't even own trainers. The last time I did any sort of exercise was ten years ago before I had any children. I have always assumed that constantly being in motion was equal to exercise but that was not the case. I needed that time for myself away from my children, work and everyday worries. I committed myself to starting a regular exercise plan, slowly but steadily as this was essential for my mind and body. I needed to get my body back into the healthiest shape in order to prevent a recurrence of cancer. Life around us was also seemingly back to normal with businesses running as usual.

With November showing its face, Covid cases around the world continued rising and the second wave became official. As neighbouring countries were going into another partial or full lockdown, Luxembourg still remained open despite the rise in cases. Understandably, the fear of catching a simple infection, let alone Covid was a terrifying thought for any cancer patient. The media reports we have been witnessing since the start of the pandemic was enough to scare anyone, cancer or not. People dying alone in isolation without their loved ones was a common scene in the media. During the first lockdown, I had a healthy immune system and like so many people my age, catching this new virus would have been no big deal. A few months later, I am being put in the category of highest vulnerability. Needless to say, that I had already pictured myself on a lonely ward with medical staff in protective gear without my loved ones, imagining the worst.

Interestingly, by November, I had also finished the bulk of this book and I started to be able to soundly sleep again. It was very healing to be able to finally just close my eyes after two years of horrid insomnia. I credit the writing of this book to this. My suppressed negative emotions are finally out, and I can sleep with no worries apparent. With the fear in the back of my mind still present, I started to research how I could learn more about my specific cancer to be able to best prevent a relapse. I had to be quicker than this aggressive cancer. It was a race against time. With no regard to cost, I investigated what tests and assays could be done to best be prepared should a relapse happen one day. One of the assays performed was a chemo-sensitivity test which would predict which chemotherapy drugs would be most efficient against my specific cancerous cells. Despite the many downfalls of this method, I was simply keen on getting data about my specific cancer that could help me in the future. Be it in a few months or a few years. I needed to be ready and be smarter than my cancer.

Only a few weeks after my last therapy, I asked to have an ultrasound. I somehow had a nagging feeling that my treatment was not aggressive enough especially since the cancer was a stage 3. Despite being treated according to the current clinical evidence-based guidelines, the fact that my tumour was of a very fast-growing type was not giving me inner peace.

Well-meaning friends kept telling me that I should now calm down and stop being pro-active as I am missing out on life's beautiful moments by giving this cancer too much thought. I should now relax for three months as 'what will be will be' and we can't change it anyway. Always listen to your instinct as it's mostly right. I understand that it is well meaning to tell a person going through cancer that 'we could all die tomorrow'. For someone actually facing their own mortality, however, such a statement is unfortunately stinging and should at best be left unsaid.

As the oncologist checked each organ on the ultrasound, he reassured me one by one that my organs looked healthy with no suspicions. As he continued, I could see in his eyes that something was wrong and that he may have spotted a mass that was not supposed to be there. This was only a few weeks past treatment. I started to get worried that this nightmare is starting all over again. How could there still be something this soon after treatment in that specific treated zone. The radiotherapy was supposed to burn my insides in that area. Was the cancer this aggressive that it did not respond to the primary and secondary treatment at all? Was this already a relapse this soon after treatment? The oncologist did not hesitate and quickly sent me for an urgent scan the next day. Up until this point, I believed this was potentially a local recurrence keeping my cancer at stage 3.

The following day at the scan, I surprisingly remained calm considering the likely bad news that may be awaiting me. Getting nuclear imaging done was now familiar to me. The staff, however, leaving the room when the machine starts does not really instil confidence in this procedure as being healthy for my body. That same day, I nervously contacted my oncologist, in order to know what the scan revealed. I needed to know whether to mentally prepare for a new battle or was it a false alarm and I could breathe a sigh of relief...for now. Despite being very busy, he kindly agreed to see me right after the scan during his chemotherapy ward rounds.

He sat me down and we looked at the images together. He showed me the apparent mass in my pelvis but unfortunately, he did not stop there. As he kept talking, my heart started racing again anticipating more bad news. I tried to listen to what he was saying but I somehow switched off when he explained that the radiologist also incidentally spotted a few suspicious nodules on my lungs. I felt that I could not breathe at that point, but I tried to remain calm enough to hear what he was saying. We agreed that the best course of action was for me to return to Germany where I had my surgery for the Gynaeco-oncologist to decide what we should do next. I spent the weekend with David, trying to distract myself from this possible worst-case scenario while already anticipating the 'what if'.

I had already somehow prepared myself mentally for the possibility of a metastatic cancer with the cancer spreading and the shock of the situation was therefore not as big as it would have been had I been living a care-free post-cancer life. That inner urge to be pro-active and getting checked beyond the regular three-monthly gynaecological follow-up, was there from the moment I knew the cancer had spread into the lymphatic system. David, on the other hand, had not prepared himself for this scenario and understandably fell from a higher hill than I did.

With this new information, I decided to sit my children down in front of our whiteboard and I pretended to be a teacher while they were writing along. I explained to them everything from scratch, I made a biology class out of the situation to lighten up the mood. I told them what cancer was, even using THE word for the first time. I described what treatment had already been done and told them that cancer can return again. I also told them that if a treatment was necessary, it would involve more medicine going into my ball under my collar bone. I reassured them that if I had to have medicine, it would be done in Luxembourg and not in Germany and that they would stay with me as long as nobody was sick. I explained to them that the medicine weakens the immune system, and that mummy needs to be extra careful especially with a new virus around. They agreed that each time one of them was sick that they would go to their father's house to sleep to protect me.

In order to somehow prepare my children for another few months of uncertainty, I sought ways of making the inevitable disruption in their little lives as smooth as I could. The day after the revelation that I would need more treatment, and that I was now most likely a stage 4 cancer patient, I took the children to an electronics store and we bought a portable gaming console. I kindly asked them whether they would let me borrow it during my chemotherapy sessions as it was very boring to sit there for hours. They gave me full permission to take their video games along with me. I also tried to prepare them for the fact that my hair will most likely fall out even more this time than the first chemotherapy rounds. In order to avoid a radical change, I let them know that once my hair falls off by itself, we'll go to the hairdresser and each of the 4 children could cut a ponytail and the lady can shave all the rest. They thought this would be a fun activity to do once the time came. I also reminded them that, like the last treatment, I will most likely experience nausea and vomiting from the medication and that I will be very tired during the next months. I had to somehow get the grounds ready as in a short time they already had too many events troubling their little stable world.

Since I had recently just started a new job, I felt very guilty for asking my employer to prolong my sick leave for the treatment ahead. I was very lucky to have found in my supervisor a very human and understanding employer who reassured me that my priority now should be my health and that they will be waiting for me with open arms once this bad spell was over. That reassurance was worth gold as I knew that this was not always a given in every workplace.

After trying to distract myself as best as I could with David on our childfree weekend, I went to the hospital for more scans in order to investigate further whether the cancer had metastasised to the lungs and possibly elsewhere. Walking down the long corridor with my bulky pink medical folder towards the imaging facility, I felt very disconnected. This could not be happening again, not this soon already. I was naturally hoping it was all just a mistake and that the scan would show no hypermetabolic activity in my cells. Deep down, I knew that this was probably not a false alarm and with the bad news piling up these past months, I did not feel like I was on a lucky strike. I felt like this was simply a logical sequence of events of not treating the primary tumour with an aggressive approach tailored to the individual case against the current clinical guidelines.

After the scan, David and I drove to Germany to get a second opinion on the case. David remained calm throughout, not showing me at any point that I should fear for my life, which in my eyes was the right strategy. Two scared people sitting together in a car for hours is not a healthy mix. Even if deep down, I knew that David was also scared of losing me to this disease. I am thankful that he remained the one that pushed me forward when I had self-doubts whether I could ever make it through. I am a lucky girl to have him by my side and with so much love given to me by my children, David and his children, I believed nothing bad could ever happen to me.

The next day, we were given the results of the multiple scans. The oncologist sat us down and we waited while he consulted the radiologist. The consensus between doctors in Luxembourg, Germany and the US was pretty clear that the lung nodules looked like metastases and the word 'incurable' hit me hard. Trying to get a biopsy from that area was too dangerous and could lead to the lungs collapsing. I did not know what to do with myself at that point. With David sitting beside me in shock, I simply listened to what the doctor had to say. I was glad to have two other ears listening as I tend to disconnect when the information gets too brutal.

I was in a state of urgency to commence treatment as soon as possible to get rid of this new issue. The doctor, however, advised me to wait a few months before starting treatment as my overall survival rate would not be changed anyway regardless of starting treatment early or late. With all due respect to my doctor, I was not going to wait for clinical symptoms such as coughing up blood to appear months down the line before attacking these cells. I just could not do the 'wait and see' approach anymore. I had to be faster than these cells. I had to do something about this as soon as possible, especially knowing how fast growing this type of cancer was.

The doctor agreed to a treatment plan that I could do in Luxembourg near my children. The drive back home was tense, but I somehow felt in control of the situation. I was happy to have been proactive enough to reveal an incidental finding despite me now most likely being considered a terminally ill patient. The cancer treatment that is given to a stage 4 patient is termed palliative. Many people are familiar with this term as being associated with optimising life quality of terminally ill patients. Nowadays, this term is not always associated with end-of-life but can also be used for treatment that is given in tandem with curative approaches. This is the definition that I was going to cling on to. Cancer is an absolute mind game. It is an invisible disease. People are walking around with cancer and they have no idea unless it is advanced enough to cause clinical symptoms. Cancer usually does not give you symptoms. It is very sneaky indeed and vigilance is key. Years can pass by without any symptoms from an initial stage 1 diagnosis to a sudden stage 4 with no warning.

That night, back home, I just could not stay away from the internet and I started searching for prognosis and survival rates of lung metastases. At best, even with treatment, those ranged from three to six months. My heart dropped and I evidently got myself into a panic mode, promising myself never to search such nonsense on the World Wide Web again. I knew better. I knew that I was me, I was unique and that was my power. That statement became my mantra whenever reality struck, and I projected myself into a morbid mood again. I have been through hell quite a few times and have come back smiling, there was no way that this cancer was going to kill me. Did this cancer not realise whose body it decided to camp in?

My children were quietly sleeping in their bed while their mother was genuinely scared for her life.

Although I had no negative emotions towards Felix at that point; being faced with a possible death sentence brought more anger and sadness towards him. The painful memory of the stress he forced upon me during these 18 months following the discovery of his adultery, which in turn caused the severe insomnia, was resurfacing again. How could it not? I slept very well during our ten years of marriage and I was suddenly in a state of chronic stress again caused by his actions.

The mere vision of him being the sole caregiver of my children was enough for me to be determined to survive this second wave. There was no way in this world that Felix would be the main parent to our beautiful children. This was never going to happen. This was my motivation to dissect this cancer, learn about its weak spots and attack it the best I could before it could attack me. I kept reassuring my children from that day on that I will always be around for them. I promised them that I will also be a grandmother and look after their own children one day. This second wave also urged me to finish this book although I knew that I would live for another 50 years at least.

Picking up my children from school was very hard that first week. Small talk with fellow parents was impossible. I could not hold it together anymore and I just cried uncontrollably in front of the school alongside other parents waiting for their children to come out. I think reality hit me at that moment that the situation was way worse than I could ever have anticipated. I felt the injustice right there. I had just started a new job, I was stable, I was in love and I was surrounded by my children and yet, something had to happen to cause turbulence in my idyllic world yet again. Was I not worthy of a quiet, trouble-free life? Why is everyone around me seemingly fine and worrying about what to cook for dinner that evening?

How could I be stuck in this parallel world totally disconnected from real life problems and fearing not to be able to see my babies grow? What if the treatment did not work? How did I go from a seemingly fit mother to a terminally ill patient in a matter of months? What if the prognosis was correct and no matter what I did, the cancer was too aggressive and would win? I was only human after all and did not have any superpowers. I hugged my children tighter that day. I kept bouncing from a state of control and power to a state of paralysing fear. My children felt the insecurity behind my big smile. They sensed the crippling fear when I self-doubted whether I would make it or not. Visiting my daughter's grave that first week was very healing and empowering. It was as if she told me that 'everything will be fine'. I somehow regained the strength I had lost after each visit. She gave me a sense of calmness, ready to tackle the next challenge ahead. I was determined to evict my unwanted subtenant with all my power.

The following week, I started the first cycle of another five months of chemotherapy. The medical staff was very pleasant, and it was nice to speak Luxembourgish at last. While checking my chemotherapy protocol on my first visit to make sure that I receive the appropriate dosage, I could not help but giggle at the comment written by the hospital pharmacist on my notes. It stated that 'the patient is complicated'. I sure was. During this whole cancer journey, I have not been the easiest of patients as I remain the critical thinking scientist that I have been trained to be.

I question everything and can't possibly be the obedient patient that is expected of me. I have been known as the complicated patient during the past months and rightly so. I must remain my own health advocate, nobody will stand for me other than myself. I am involved in my own care and it is surely not a one-way relationship. The patient, together with the doctor, needs to be able to make an informed decision about their own care, which is sadly not always the case. Surprisingly, despite the new storm hitting me, I am still able to sleep soundly. This, for me, is the biggest sign of emotional healing that has happened thanks to this liberating book that I am currently writing. It somehow needed to be written to get everything out and start a new life chapter.

The analysis of my primary tumour revealed that this cancer was a sporadic event. This was very important to me as it underlines the fact that there was no genetic component to the disease. In addition, it shows that there is no malfunction in my cells that would make more cells unable to repair themselves. This cancer is purely stress-induced. The extreme insomnia over 18 months has severely weakened my immune system to the point that it could not do its job properly anymore and the cells at some point started going off track, multiplying indefinitely until a tumour was formed. It was great to realise that the sleep issue had resolved itself and that I got out of this vicious cycle thanks to this book. One of the main elements that has made this cancer thrive was the intense chronic stress following the divorce and this too was now eliminated. I am now in a calmer, positive state than I have ever been in my life. Despite being in the middle of a new scary chapter, I feel in control and content. I regard my cancer as another PhD thesis that I can dedicate all my knowledge and skills to. I do not see cancer as this invisible monster that can hurt me anymore. I see it all more technical and will therefore spend money on analysing it as much as I can in order to get rid of it in the most efficient way with the lowest toxicity to my body.

Shortly after finishing the first treatment, I came across a book written by Jane McLelland. This was not only an inspiring long term cancer survivor story. This woman took the concept of 'being your own health advocate' to a whole new level. I was inspired despite being skeptical at first. Now at a potential stage 4, what did I have to lose? I went against all my pre-formed professional convictions and gave this approach a shot. The concept is very evidence-based and is to be used in conjunction with conventional treatment such as chemotherapy, radiotherapy, surgery, targeted therapy and immunotherapy. It is not an alternative treatment that dismisses the pharmaceutical drugs, but it is a smart mix between natural substances, pharmaceutical drugs and conventional cancer treatment while being evidence-based and not simply made up.

The online platform and interactive online course that Jane has brought to life is what any cancer patient needs, especially in moments of desperation. We all need to see positive progress stories. Dr Martin Inderbitzin, a neuroscientist and a cancer survivor who has defied all odds of survival has created a great project interviewing worldwide cancer survivors. This is exactly what keeps patients going despite the horrid side effects of the treatment. Especially with a terminal cancer diagnosis when doctors have already written a patient off by predicting their grim prognosis counted in months. Personally, I do not understand what added value this information could possibly bring to a patient. All it does is remove any hope and fighting spirit that may still be there. I understand that perhaps doctors want to make sure that the patient gets their 'affairs in order' if they know that their expiry date is imminent, but I totally disagree with this approach. Doctors are human, patients are individuals and not statistics. How many patients have surpassed their predicted prognosis and are in good health today against all odds? Why not me?

I increasingly surrounded myself with people that had gone through cancer and were ready to share their positive stories with me. We sometimes cross path with people for a reason. I was seeking hope that I was going to make it out the other end. Through a friend, I got to know a beautiful young woman by the name of Anne-Sophie. She is radiant. The positive strength in her sparkling hazel eyes was not to be missed. She had gone through hell and back and was sitting opposite me many years later to tell the tale. She became one of many people that I admired for their continuous positive perseverance despite immense adversity. The healing power of the positive mind is not to be underestimated.

Working in clinical research, I was very familiar with the placebo effect. I truly believe in the power of positive thinking impacting our healing. This phenomenon is commonly observed in randomised clinical trials in which a group of people receives the experimental drug while the other group receives an inert substance. The mere belief of the placebo group that they are given the actual drug is enough to produce a favourable effect on their disease evolution. The opposite is also true and equally as powerful. If a patient has already given up before even trying simply because the doctor in white has given them THE speech, then the body will evidently follow.

The cancer patient needs more than prayers and miracles. They need to be pro-active and disobedient. They need to be taking charge. Succumbing to the label of a diagnosis and prognosis should never be the viable option. Evidently, not everyone will be in that category and that is fine too. There should be no pressure in any way on the patient to 'keep fighting'. It is fine if the patient is tired and can't handle the treatment anymore. It is OK if the patient decides that they have had enough and can't be 'strong' anymore as expected by their loved ones. I fully understand that aspect too and it does not mean in any way that the patient has failed. On the contrary, it takes immense courage to recognise one's limits and somehow be content with the end despite the pushy expectations. I could not allow myself to slip into that category for one moment. I was not going to let a bunch of cells in my body rob me of my existence. This was not in my cards.

Anne-Sophie reminded me of a very important point. The term 'incurable' does not mean anything really. Just like diabetes and asthma are incurable, so is cancer. By changing our perspective on the disease, we can regard it as a chronic condition that needs lifelong management just like any other disease that can't fully be cured. Vigilance is key when it comes to recurrence prevention. The terminology used in the cancer community resembles war language. We fight a battle against an enemy. On the news we hear a celebrity losing their battle against cancer. Unfortunately, there is a big portion of luck at play when it comes to surviving this disease. The fact that a person does not make it, reflects in no way that they have not 'fought' hard enough. There is so much that still needs to be understood that it will take time to fully decipher this disease. What works for one person, may not be adequate for the next person as many other inherent factors play a role in the manifestation and progression of the disease. We are all unique and should therefore be treated as such.

Since I had promised myself to be more vigilant about my future health, I underwent various medical screening tests in order to avoid any surprises later on. I was done with surprises at that point. I needed to be in full control of my health even though one can never really know what is happening inside, prevention is key. Following a colonoscopy, a mammography and a full dermatological body check, I thought further. During the past months, I have been repeatedly asked about my family medical history and I realised I did not have that information, which could be crucial in my disease prevention. I always replied with 'no available information' when asked whether there was cancer in my family. I did not have access to this information, which was key in being pro-active about my future health.

Before attending my genetic counselling session in order to check for genetic mutations that could predispose me to breast cancer, I did something I never thought I would ever get to do in my lifetime. The laboratory needed to know whether there was a family history of breast or ovarian cancer in my family. If that genetic test came back positive, I was ready to undergo a preventive double mastectomy. I did not want any more surprises. I then decided to contact Denise in order to find out. After 12 years of silence, I wrote her a message specifying this one request of information, nothing more. It was a very factual emotionless message. She replied saying that apart from our mother being a little tired these days, there was no known female family member with this condition. She gave me my mother's phone number and asked me to call if I wanted to ask anything else.

Since I had nothing to lose but only to win, I took all my courage and dialled the number given to me. I was very calm for someone who has not spoken to her mother in 12 years. The last time I called her she insisted on me retracting all I had said at the police station and asked me to go to church to confess for what I had done to Nicolas. I never thought I would ever speak to her again. As the phone was ringing, I contemplated whether to hang up or not. What if Nicolas picked up first? I decided to hang up if he was the one answering the phone. Denise picked up the phone and asked me who I was. I said 'Mary'. She answered 'One moment please' as if she was a secretary passing me on to the director. My mother got on the phone and said 'Hello, who is speaking?'. I answered 'Mary'. She shockingly asked 'my daughter?'. I said 'yes'. She said 'I miss you so much'. I could not reply to that. I went straight into the factual conversation.

I could hear Nicolas talking in the background. Talking to her meant also talking to this family behind her, she was not an individual. I asked her whether there was a history of breast or ovarian cancer in her family. She said that she had a painful lump in her breast for a long time and she was given an antibiotic to treat it for three months. I then asked her whether it was an infection, she replied the doctor had told her it was cancer. I was shocked, I did not know what to do with this information. I asked her if it was cancer then it is definitely not an antibiotic that she should be taking.

I insisted that she quickly needed surgery and/or chemotherapy and if she did not do so, she could soon be dead. She seemingly got upset despite her being a doctor. I was not surprised that my mother did not realise the seriousness of her situation while being on heavy medication for the past thirty years. She was at the full mercy of her family and I could not help her. How did she have cancer and was not getting any chemotherapy? How was that even possible? Did Nicolas find a golden opportunity to finally get rid of her? How did her other children, most of them in the medical profession not do anything about it? How is being 'a little tired' equal to 'breast cancer'? How long did she have this lump for?

My heart was very broken, and I started crying at the thought of her being left to die by her own family. I did not feel any negative emotions towards her. She did not deserve this life of misery. She was married to a tyrant and found herself in a situation that she could not get out of. I felt very powerless. I could not go any further without waking up the devil behind her. Perhaps my empathy was ever more increased as my mother and I were now unfortunately sharing a common battle, only she was not fighting at all. I pictured her in pain in her final moments while slowly being internally invaded by this cancer. However, despite my immense sadness for her situation, I felt relief to have brought her some happiness with her hearing my voice. Perhaps it would be the last time in her life. I definitely found closure in that moment.

Feeling well after that first chemotherapy session, I decided to visit the medical wig shop. I took David along on this somewhat unusual Saturday afternoon date. It was very special for both of us. That trip was bearing a very deep connection. I tried on many different wigs of dark brown colour. I tried the synthetic ones and the natural ones. Despite it being a very emotional trip for David and myself, we had a great laugh. At that moment, I was sure that no matter how the treatment will physically impact on me, that this man, sitting right there watching me try on wig after wig, would find me pretty. I had no doubt that his loving smile was genuine. In my dark self-doubt moments, David was right there to reassure me that everything will be fine and that there was absolutely no alternative to that. I truly believed that nothing bad could happen to me in that moment. I was simply happy in that present moment, regardless of the past and future. That same day, David gifted me a beautiful bracelet with blue and white sparkles. This bracelet was going to be my lucky charm and safely get me through the coming difficult months.

A few chemotherapy cycles in, I had a good scan, which can only be described as a feeling of rebirth. Even though, the future is uncertain, for now I conclude this somewhat strange year with a bald head and a happy heart. My oncologist was very pleased and positive, which in turn helps me to keep my positivity up.

Chapter Six

No one is you and that is your power, own it.
David Grohl

Everything will be just fine.

I am a firm believer that things happen for a reason at a specific time. We can't force things. We don't know why an adversity may be happening today and how it will impact on us in the future while only time will tell. I embrace the uncertainty and believe that brighter days are waiting for me. I was given these challenging situations for a reason that I did not know the meaning of at the time. The writing of this book has brought me closure in so many ways. I do not hold any negative emotions anymore. I am finally free and can give my full attention to what matters most in life. My daughter, who is my guardian angel is watching over me. Not only will I survive, but I will thrive against all odds. Nobody is me and that is my power. By the time of publication, while reading my first draft, I was conflicted with myself. The perfectionist in me needed to submit a sound manuscript as if I had written a scientific article. The fearful mother in me, however, felt that these pages written while the trauma was happening preserved their authenticity because of it.

Today, I feel very grateful to still be standing and smiling. Over the years, I have developed the tools to be able to see the good in the most difficult situations and actively contribute to my happiness and that of my children. I will be the one in charge of my survival by not letting life's uninvited struggles step all over me, however hard it may be. That is a conscious decision. Tomorrow is a new day and whether it will be a good one or not, I have the power to make it better than the previous one. Life is a precious gift that only you can determine the fate of. Your attitude towards the unfortunate obstacles that hit you is fully in your hands. Take advantage of the power of the positive mind, you are stronger than you think you could ever be. Smile to yourself even if you don't feel like it. This sends a signal to the brain that everything is fine. No matter how many of those adversity stamps you're given on your forehead, it has within, the ability of great expansion. Within each of us lies fierceness, confidence and resilience. I am not special in any way. Believe that you can, and your body will follow.

I truly believe that if you do good in life, good things happen to you in return. I have always lived by this and that definitely gives me a sense of inner peace. Regardless of the number of hardships I have had and are yet to receive in the future, I will remain kind and trusting. Smiling never hurt anyone. It is free and it is definitely underutilised in our current rushed society. Perhaps that random smile will unknowingly make a stranger's day. Life goes on and when (not if) I survive cancer, I will vow to help others who have been, or currently are, in my shoes. I am here to tell you that you too can make it through. Let go, forgive and even though it is very difficult to forget, finding closure by making peace with all of the negative emotions is the only way forward, there is no alternative. Life is very beautiful if you open your eyes and actually stop and see.

With all my courage to you,
Mary

Glossary of Medical Terms

Adrenaline	a hormone secreted by the adrenal glands, also known as the 'fight-or flight' hormone. It is released, amongst others, in response to a stressful threatening situation
Chemosensitivity assay	a laboratory test that measures the number of cancer cells killed by chemotherapy. The test is performed in order to determine the best chemotherapeutic agent to use against a specific tumour
Chemotherapy	chemical substances used to kill or slow the progression of cancer cells
Cortisol	the body's primary stress hormone. It is released, amongst others, in response to threatening situations
CT scan	computerised tomography scan using computers and rotating X-ray machines to create cross-sectional images of the body
'Fight or flight' response.	the body's acute response to stress characterised by a racing heart rate, faster breathing and a tense body posture, ready to take action
Immunotherapy	type of cancer treatment using the body's immune system to fight the disease
Lymphatic system	network of tissues and organs that help the body get rid of toxins and fight infections
Lymph nodes	small glands that filter lymph (clear fluid flowing through the lymphatic system)
Metastases	the development of secondary cancerous growth away from the primary cancer
MRI scan	magnetic resonance imaging using very strong magnetic fields and radio waves to produce detailed images of tissues and organs

NED	No evidence of disease
Off-label	the use of a medicine for a condition beyond the condition for which the medicine was originally approved
Pap smear	routine procedure to collect cells within the cervix to detect precancerous cells
PET scan	positron emission tomography scan produces coloured 3D images of the metabolic activity within the cells
Post-partum	the period following the birth of an infant
Prognosis	the expected development of a disease
REM sleep	rapid eye movement sleep is one of the sleep phases during which memory is thought to be consolidated
Radiotherapy	cancer treatment using ionising radiation to kill cancer cells
Survival rate	often stated as a 5-year period after which a percentage of people in a group is still alive following the initial diagnosis or treatment
Targeted therapy	type of cancer treatment that targets specific genes or proteins involved in the growth and survival of cancer cells
White blood cells	cells of the immune system involved in protecting the body against infections

Useful Contacts

Author's contact: dr.mary.faltz@gmail.com

Website: www.maryfaltz.com
Facebook: Dr. Mary Faltz
Instagram: dr_mary_faltz
Twitter: Dr. Mary Faltz
Linkedin: Mary Faltz, MPharm, PhD

Useful links and contacts (Luxembourg)

Femmes en détresse
www.fed.lu
organisation@fed.lu

Child protection
www.childprotection.lu

ECPAT
www.ecpat.lu
ecpat-luxembourg@ecpat.lu

Police grand-ducale 'Protection de la Jeunesse'
Tel: 12321

BEE SECURE Stopline
www.stopline.bee-secure.lu
BEE SECURE Helpline
Tel: 26 64 05 44

Kanner Jugend Telefon (KJT)
Tel: 116 111
www.kjt.lu

Ombuds-Comité fir d'Rechter vum Kand (ORK)
www.ork.lu

Office national de l'enfance (ONE)
www.one.public.lu

Service central d'assistance sociale (SCAS) - service d'aide aux victimes
Tel: 47 58 21 1

SOS Détresse
Tel: 45 45 45

ALUPSE
www.alupse.lu

Fondation Cancer
Tel: 45 30 331
fondation@cancer.lu

Centre de réhabilitation post oncologique du Château de Colpach
Tel: 27 55 43 00

Groupes Sportifs Oncologiques
info@sportifsoncologiques.lu
Tel: 691 12 12 07
Cérémonie des étoiles- Maternité G-D Charlotte
chl@chl.lu

Thank you for leaving a review of this book online. If we all contribute to reaching a wider audience then we'll help raise awareness about childhood sexual abuse and empower others who find themselves facing adversity.

My Daily Gratitude Journal

DATE:

5 things I'm grateful for:
1. _____
2. _____
3. _____
4. _____
5. _____

4 things I'm looking forward to:
1. _____
2. _____
3. _____
4. _____

3 things I accomplished today:
1. _____
2. _____
3. _____

2 people I'm grateful to have in my life:
1. _____
2. _____

1 amazing thing that happened this week:
_____
_____
_____

LOVEOURMINDS.COM

www.ingramcontent.com/pod-product-compliance
Lightning Source LLC
Chambersburg PA
CBHW071621080526
44588CB00010B/1216